WORKING TOWARD EXCELLENCE

Praise for
Working Toward Excellence

Working Toward Excellence has captured my attention in a big way. It is filled with valuable and practical information. It will make a major difference in your life.

Pat Williams, Orlando Magic senior vice president, author of *Leadership Excellence*

Dr. Buyer's excellent book weaves together thoughts, stories, and quotes from top performers in music, business, and sports to help you achieve excellence. This is an inspiring read for any performer who wants to take their game to the next level.

Jeff Janssen, author of *The Seven Secrets of Successful Coaches* and *Championship Team Building*

Paul's book is a treasure trove of great advice and counsel about working toward excellence. He has done a masterful job in researching great leaders and their approach to excellence. I believe it is definitely a "must book" and have provided a copy to all of our Head Coaches for their study and evaluation of how to work toward excellence, not only personally, but certainly for their teams and student-athletes.

Terry Don Phillips, Director of Athletics, Clemson University

In *Working Toward Excellence,* Paul Buyer takes a fresh look at an age old challenge: how to be the very best you can be. I was particularly engaged by Paul's use of unusual examples of excellence from The Cleveland Orchestra to Augusta National Golf Club. This is a book that grabs your attention, holds it, and motivates you to take action.

Joe Calloway, author of *Becoming a Category of One*

Paul Buyer, in his inimitable style, has created a really excellent book on "working toward excellence" . . . what a perfect title! This book is a valuable read for anyone at any stage in their journey toward success, quality and excellence in their lives.

Gary Cook, Professor Emeritus of Music, University of Arizona; Past-President, Percussive Arts Society

Dr. Buyer has provided us with a handbook for the pursuit of excellence—not just in music, but in life. His eight "uncommon values" are valuable touchstones in a remarkable book that should provide an inspiration for anyone who reads it.

Dr. Richard E. Goodstein, Dean, College of Architecture, Arts and Humanities, Clemson University

Dr. Paul Buyer articulates and defines what is inherently indefinable. The author provides logical and concrete insights into the process of becoming excellent. *Working*

Toward Excellence is a must read for anyone interested in achieving excellence in their field.

Dr. Michael Sammons, Director of Percussion, University of South Alabama

Working Toward Excellence is an exceptional new book about what it takes to stand out and achieve uncommon success in your industry. By breaking down values critical to achieving at a high level such as hunger, effort, leadership, time, and others, this book literally shows you how to work toward excellence and achieve it.

Craig Duswalt, speaker, author and creator of the RockStar System For Success, www.CraigDuswalt.com

Also by Paul Buyer

Marching Bands and Drumlines:
Secrets of Success from the Best of the Best
Meredith Music Publications
www.paulbuyer.com

WORKING
TOWARD
EXCELLENCE

8 Values for Achieving
Uncommon Success in Work and Life

PAUL BUYER

NEW YORK

Working Toward Excellence

8 Values for Achieving Uncommon Success in Work and Life

ISBN 9781614481768 paperback
ISBN 9781614481775 eBook
Library of Congress Control Number: 2011943962

Morgan James Publishing
The Entrepreneurial Publisher
5 Penn Plaza, 23rd Floor, New York City, New York 10001
(212) 655-5470 office • (516) 908-4496 fax
www.MorganJamesPublishing.com

CONTENTS

ACKNOWLEDGMENTS

This book is a culmination of a relentless pursuit of excellence in my work and life, and my sincere and genuine desire to share these lessons with others. For those who know me well, I hope I have made you proud in this pursuit, for without your love, support, and encouragement, this book would not have been written.

First, I want to thank my wife April for inspiring me every day. Her giving heart and uncommon effort for making a difference in the lives of others is truly remarkable. I am a better person because of her and look forward to many more years of working toward excellence together.

I want to thank my mother Andrea, father Richard, brother Jason, sister Kennedy, grandmother Rose, and stepfather Ken for their constant love and support, as well as my stepmother Kris for allowing me to tell her story of perseverance.

I am forever grateful and indebted to my teachers and mentors Gary Cook, Erwin Mueller, and Michael Balter for showing me what I am capable of and instilling in me the eight values discussed in this book.

Thank you to my friend Mike Sammons for our many philosophical conversations about excellence and mediocrity, and to my friends Tony Stapleton and Larry Sloan for their support and encouragement on and off the golf course.

I would like to thank my students, past and present, for making me a better teacher and allowing me to help them work toward excellence and reach their potential. They are truly the inspiration for this book.

To my colleagues at Clemson University: Rick Goodstein, David Hartmann, Mickey Harder, Linda Li-Bleuel, Mark Spede, Justin Durham, Bruce Whisler, Tim Hurlburt, Mark Hosler, Dan Rash, Andrew Levin, and Linda Dzuris. Your collective dedication to excellence has successfully created a culture of collaboration and growth in our department.

I would like to recognize and thank my editor Amanda Rooker of Amanda Rooker Editing and the team at Morgan James for their outstanding work on this book: David Hancock, Founder of Morgan James Publishing; Rick Frishman, Publisher; Cindy Sauer, Director of Administration; Dave Sauer, Senior Author Liason; Jim Howard, Publishing Director; Bethany Marshall, Marketing Manager; Lyza Poulin, Author Relations Manager; Jaye Pratt, Interior Design Consultant; Margo Toulouse, Author Relations Manager; and Kim Spano, Author Relations Manager.

Finally, I am grateful for two mentors whom I have never met, but whose influence nonetheless ignited my passion for excellence and helped guide me toward reaching my leadership potential: John Wooden and John C. Maxwell. Their wisdom is peppered throughout these pages, and I hope their words inspire you like they inspire me.

Paul Buyer

INTRODUCTION

Starting today, let's banish the philosophy of mediocrity. No matter what your occupation or endeavor, excellence is what you and your people create on your turf. It can be done and it is done. There is no excuse for not getting on with it among your people.

Tom Peters, business author and consultant

This book is about working toward excellence in any endeavor. It is about reaching your full potential, being the best of which you are capable, and developing a low tolerance for mediocrity. It is about raising your standards and expectations for yourself and those you lead, and about taking your work as far as you can. As *SUCCESS Magazine* founder and thought leader Orison Swett Marden states, "Just make up your mind at the very outset that your work is going to stand for quality... that you are going to stamp a superior quality upon everything that goes out of your hands; that whatever you do shall bear the hallmark of excellence."

Do those words inspire you? They certainly inspire me! I believe working toward excellence is a noble goal in anything you do. Working toward excellence is a wonderful way to live your life and provides a constant source of motivation and inspiration. Sometimes we achieve it, and sometimes we fall short, but if we always *work toward* it, we will not have any regrets. Excellence is compelling, in part, because it is hard to achieve. The philosopher Plato even said, "Excellent things are rare." But sometimes excellence is not expected. Sometimes the bar is not very high. Sometimes good enough is good enough. But for those who aspire for greatness, *good enough is not.* So, what does excellence look like? Why should we pursue it? And what values must we master to achieve it?

DEFINING EXCELLENCE

According to the *Collins English Dictionary,* excellence is "the state or quality of excelling or being exceptionally good; extreme merit; superiority." Other definitions include "of the highest quality," "greatness," "at an elite level," "being outstanding," "top-shelf," "first-rate," and "mastery of your work." Former Secretary of Health, Education, and Welfare John W. Gardner defined excellence as simply "doing ordinary things extraordinarily well."

My interest in excellence comes from being a music professor at Clemson University, where I serve as Director of Percussion and Director of Music in the Department of Performing Arts. Prior to teaching at Clemson, I was a high school band director in Garland, Texas, just outside of Dallas. My musical background includes teaching and playing a variety of percussion instruments such as snare drum, marimba, vibraphone, xylophone, timpani, drumset, cymbals, bass drum, and steel drums, as well as playing in marching band, drum and bugle corps, wind ensembles, jazz ensembles, and professional symphony orchestras.

Like many professions, music is a field that demands excellence. Jim Collins, in his book *Good to Great and the Social Sectors,* cites The Cleveland Orchestra as a "great organization," which he defined as "one that delivered superior performance and makes a distinctive impact over a long period of time." Collins says, "[Conductor] Tom Morris could not precisely measure artistic excellence, but that does not change the fact that artistic excellence *is* the primary definition of performance for The Cleveland Orchestra. Nor does it change the extreme discipline with which The Cleveland Orchestra held itself accountable for playing the most challenging classical music with supreme artistic excellence, and doing so even better with each passing year, guided by the ... goal of becoming recognized as one of the three greatest orchestras in the world."

Another good example of musical excellence is the Dallas Brass. Long admired for being one of the world's finest musical ensembles, the Dallas Brass is a professional brass ensemble featuring six players on trumpets, horn, trombone, tuba, and drumset/percussion. Always searching for inspiration and sharing their joy of music, the sextet enjoys asking fellow musicians to describe a "wow moment" that had a significant impact on their musical development. Simply stated, wow moments are those jaw-dropping moments when you are so inspired by excellence that you become determined to do whatever it takes to be that good.

In describing one of his own wow moments during a clinic with Clemson music students, Dallas Brass trumpet player D.J. Barraclough explains:

It's that factor of excellence that seems to captivate our attention. In every wow moment we've ever collected from any of the clinics we've given, there's always one element. And that is what was witnessed was so excellent, it made the person observing want to be more like that, want to become what they had just witnessed. That's the magic and inspiration and why those wow moments are so powerful because if you will align yourself with that—particularly right before you go to practice—you take an inspired "you" to the practice room. You're going to expect more out of yourself, and you're going to insist on getting more out of yourself. And there's something really powerful about that.

Although musical excellence is subjective and difficult to measure, it is often based on specific factors such as ensemble precision, balance and blend, intonation, phrasing, musicianship, interpretation, emotional expression, and aesthetic experience. Not surprisingly, this standard goes way beyond playing the music correctly with right notes and rhythms. In fact, I always tell my students that learning the notes is the first step, not the last.

An excellent musical performance also contains synergy, chemistry, and continuity among the performers. According to drummer Dave Weckl on his album *Synergy,* "[Synergy is] the action of two or more substances to achieve an effect of which each is individually incapable." True musical excellence, then, contains synergy—the dynamic interaction of several seasoned musicians coming together to create something they cannot create on their own. To achieve synergy, everyone collectively must care about the music and each other, and strive toward a common goal of communicating the composer's intentions and connecting with the listener in a very powerful way.

As a musician, my personal standard of excellence is based on something I heard conductor Dennis Fisher from the University of North Texas say many years ago: "Forty percent of the music is written down; sixty percent is not." What I take this to mean is that the written page is not music. It is simply a white piece of paper with black notes on it. Music comes from your instrument and, even more so, yourself. Go beyond the page.

One of my greatest joys and challenges of teaching is trying to instill in each of my students a hunger, passion, and respect for the process that excellence requires. Too often, students—and people in general—are not willing to do the things necessary to achieve excellence. They look for shortcuts, ways to beat the system, and lack accountability for their results. Why aspire for more when your work is good enough? Remember, though, that good enough is a mindset just like excellence, and when we become satisfied with that mindset, the traits of complacency, mediocrity, and apathy slowly become the habits that shape our work and lives.

Throughout these pages, I will present eight uncommon values necessary to achieve excellence. They are uncommon because the truth is that only a small percentage of people are willing to do what it takes to get to this level. Although there are other values that can also impact your success, these eight have risen to the top from over twenty years of research and experience leading individuals and teams. It is important to remember that these eight values are within your control. They are the choices and decisions you make every day.

THE EIGHT VALUES

According to Vince Lombardi Jr., "Values come in two forms: *espoused* and *practiced*. The leader's challenge is to bring these two into alignment." What does this mean for you? If you want to work toward excellence, it is not enough to promote these values and simply agree that they are important. You have to practice them—every day—and make them part of who you are.

Value 1 is HUNGER.

Hunger has to do with your level of desire, passion, drive, initiative, and ability to be proactive and self-motivated. It has to do with *wanting* excellence, something that is intrinsic and cannot be taught. As legendary Alabama football coach Bear Bryant once said, "The only thing that counts is your dedication to the game. You run on your own fuel; it comes from within you."

Value 2 is EFFORT.

Effort refers to your work ethic, focus, and ability to execute at a high level. In addition to hard work, effort has to do with your self-discipline, mental toughness, and commitment to doing your best. Entrepreneur and author Jim Rohn said, "You don't get paid for the hour. You get paid for the value you bring to the hour."

Value 3 is PROCESS.

Process focuses on the journey, not the destination. Like writing a book, teaching a class, practicing for a recital, or anything else in life that requires time to execute at a high level, process is all about your preparation. Darren Hardy said, "It's not the big things that add up in the end; it's the hundreds, thousands, or millions of little things that separate the ordinary from the extraordinary."

Value 4 is QUALITY.

Like Orison Swett Marden stated in the introduction, quality stands for something. It stands for excellence. Whether attending a concert, dining at a restaurant, or buying a new product, quality is the constant companion of excellence. Former Apple CEO Steve Jobs stated, "Be a yardstick of quality. Some people aren't used to an environment where excellence is expected."

Value 5 is CONSISTENCY.

Consistency refers to repeatedly doing the things that will put you in a position to succeed. When inconsistency occurs, "count-ability" suffers, which is your ability to count on someone or something to deliver what you expect. Be careful not to underestimate the value of consistency when working toward excellence. As the great philosopher Aristotle said, "We are what we repeatedly do. Excellence, then, is not an act, but a habit."

Value 6 is LEADERSHIP.

To achieve excellence in any endeavor, strong leadership is a prerequisite, as most things in life require the collaborative power of others. Author and leadership expert John C. Maxwell states, "Leadership ability is the lid that determines a person's level of effectiveness." Raise your lid. The best way to realize your true potential is to improve your leadership skills.

Value 7 is TIME.

Often overlooked and taken for granted, how you use and value your time has an enormous impact on your work. Those who work toward excellence—and achieve it—excel at time management and organization. Legendary coach John Wooden said, "If you don't have time to do it right, when will you have time to do it over?"

Value 8 is PERSEVERANCE.

Perseverance is the persistence, resiliency, and inner strength we need to move forward during tough times. When we face adversity head on and refuse to give up, that resolve nudges us closer to success. Boxing legend Muhammad Ali said, "Champions are made from something they have deep inside them...they have to have the skill and the will. But the will must be stronger than the skill."

EXCELLENCE, NOT PERFECTION

It is important to make a distinction between excellence and perfection. Perfection, while a worthy goal, is not realistic. It stifles creativity and creates fear of making a mistake. As psychologist and author Harriet Braiker put it, "Striving for excellence motivates you; striving for perfection is demoralizing."

In music, for example, a perfect performance—one void of any mistakes—tends to result in a safe, technical, and musically unsatisfying product. Perfection also lacks many of the intangible qualities that make music great such as emotion, expressiveness, and communication. I constantly ask my students to work toward excellence, not perfection. It takes the pressure off, allows them to relax, and gives them the freedom to play with more passion, risk, and vulnerability. As the saying goes, "Shoot for the moon. Even if you miss, you'll land among the stars."

SUSTAINING EXCELLENCE

The eight values of hunger, effort, process, quality, consistency, leadership, time, and perseverance act both independently and collectively as you strive to produce uncommon work and live an uncommon life. Each value in and of itself is powerful and capable of having a significant impact on your quest for excellence. Together, the eight values become an indomitable force, leaving no stone unturned and putting you in the best position to succeed.

There is a huge difference, however, between achieving excellence once in a while and sustaining it over time. We often hear of CEOs who have great turnarounds, coaches who have great seasons, and artists who have great performances, only to fall back into the mainstream of mediocrity soon after. The ability to sustain excellence long term—despite changes in personnel, talent, resources, and leadership—is what truly separates the best from everybody else.

A highly respected and admired leader today who has sustained excellence is Duke Basketball Coach and United States National Head Coach Mike Krzyzewski. On the 2011 ESPN special *Difference Makers: Life Lessons,* Coach K was asked, "A lot of guys are able to build teams that win for a season, or two, or an era. What's the most important thing about sustaining excellence?" Here's his response:

> I think you have to develop a culture or an environment and make everyone who's a part of your program realize that you're on a continuum; it's not one season, whether you won the whole thing or didn't win as much as you would like, that your pursuit of excellence is never going to change. It's never going to change, whatever happens with your record or whoever is in the uniforms that are representing your institution. It's called having a standard of excellence that goes on forever. That means you can't look back. That's one of the cool things about coaching. You've got to be excited about the thing in the windshield, not the rearview mirror.

Krzyzewski has been head coach at Duke since 1980, winning four NCAA national championships and leading USA Basketball to Olympic gold at the 2008 Summer Games in Beijing. Leaders like Coach K and many others in this book work toward excellence by looking out the windshield and living out these values on the road of life. Are you ready to join them?

1

Hunger

You cannot push anyone up the ladder unless he is willing to climb a little.

Andrew Carnegie, business magnate
and philanthropist

The first value you must develop if you are going to work toward excellence is *hunger*. Hunger refers to *wanting* to achieve excellence. Hunger is an intrinsic quality, and is up to the individual to find for him or herself. If you are not hungry, if you are not passionate, if you do not want to excel and succeed, don't worry—you won't. But if you do, if you truly want to achieve something significant and meaningful, you can, but you have to be hungry.

Not only must you *want* excellence, you must be *willing* to work for it, and even more importantly, you must be *eager* to do whatever is necessary to accomplish your goal. Hunger helps push you through the tough times and inevitable adversity that will accompany your road to greatness. Hunger strengthens your perseverance, persistence, and sacrifice. It is simply essential for making things happen.

There are four characteristics of people who exhibit hunger: they are proactive, they begin with the end in mind, they are self-motivated, and they exhibit desire. Let's take a closer look at these characteristics as they relate to your hunger and success.

BE PROACTIVE

"Be Proactive" is the first habit Stephen Covey writes about in his bestseller, *The Seven Habits of Highly Effective People.* What does being proactive actually mean?

Covey says being proactive means taking responsibility for your life. It means taking action, showing initiative, making things happen, not blaming others, and not making excuses. Being proactive comes down to making a choice. According to Covey, "Your life doesn't just 'happen.' Whether you know it or not, it is carefully designed by you—or carelessly designed by you. It is, after all, your choice....Proactive people recognize that they are 're-sponse-able.' They don't blame circumstances [and] conditions...for their behavior." Hall of Fame football coach Vince Lombardi said, "It is time to stand up for the doer, the achiever, the one who sets out to do something and does it," and educator Marva Collins remarked, "Success doesn't come to you...you go get it."

I remember my dad always telling me when I was looking for summer jobs, "Paul, they're not going to come to you and knock on the front door. You have to go out and apply." He was right—as usual! Be proactive, make things happen, and start taking responsibility for your life.

BEGIN WITH THE END IN MIND

The second habit of highly effective people, according to Covey, is to "Begin with the End in Mind." Without question, this habit is one of the biggest differentiators between successful and unsuccessful people. To begin with the end in mind effectively, one must be proactive in establishing a game plan and *work backwards,* visualizing the end result and working toward excellence every single day.

For musicians, nothing is more important to achieving excellence than purposeful, deliberate, and consistent practice. Several years ago, one of my students asked me a question that I will never forget: "Dr. Buyer, how do I become a great player?" What a loaded question! After thinking about it for a few minutes, this is what I came up with: "Well, first of all, you have to have a great semester every semester. To have a great semester, you have to have a great lesson every week. And to have a great lesson every week, you have to have a great practice session every day." I felt like I nailed it, like Ponce de Leon discovering the Fountain of Youth. My student nodded in agreement. Learning was taking place. I then remembered a quote from author John C. Maxwell that reinforced that teachable moment: "The secret of your success is determined by your daily agenda."

As Professor of Music and Director of Percussion at Clemson University, I have had many students over the years—some who reached their potential and some who unfortunately did not. Which path a student chose to follow always came down to their work ethic, self-discipline, commitment, and hunger, as well as their ability to be proactive and begin with the end in mind.

BECOME SELF-MOTIVATED

As an educator, I have always been fascinated with the subject of motivation. I love to hear great coaches, teachers, and leaders give speeches to motivate their people to perform at their best. I believe one of my responsibilities is to motivate my students and get them excited about music, percussion, and working toward excellence. I engage my students by inspiring them through my passion, believing in them, and challenging them to reach their potential. But to develop a *hunger* for excellence and achievement, they have to become self-motivated and not depend on others to motivate them.

The ability to motivate oneself is called *intrinsic motivation*. According to Wikipedia, "Intrinsic motivation refers to motivation that is driven by an interest or enjoyment in the task itself, and exists within the individual rather than relying on any external pressure." In contrast, "Extrinsic motivation comes from outside of the individual. Common extrinsic motivations are rewards like money and grades, coercion, and threat of punishment. Competition is in general extrinsic because it encourages the performer to win and beat others, not to enjoy the intrinsic rewards of the activity."

I first learned the difference between intrinsic and extrinsic motivation as a member of the Star of Indiana Drum and Bugle Corps. Because we played over thirty shows that summer, it was common to perform two nights in a row. I vividly remember one such occasion. Our first show was outstanding, but we finished second. Everyone was upset and depressed. The following night, we did not play our best, but we won the show. Everyone was happy, celebrating the victory. The response to these two shows had a profound impact on me. It bothered me that some of my peers preferred playing a subpar show and winning to playing an excellent show and losing. The competitive result took priority over the quality of our performance.

Drum corps taught me the values of competition and how to become self-motivated to achieve excellence. From that point forward, I would not allow judges or other people or things outside my control to motivate me. Instead, I would find the motivation within myself, setting my own bar, expectations, and standards for success.

Author Daniel Pink explores intrinsic and extrinsic motivation in his book *Drive: The Surprising Truth about What Motivates Us.* Pink explains the difference:

> We have a biological drive, and we have a reward and punishment drive. But human beings also have a third drive. We do things because we enjoy doing them or because they are the right things to do or because they contribute to the world. Science shows that this intrinsic drive is the pathway to performance. The secret to high performance is that unseen intrinsic drive, the drive to do things because they matter, and I believe that includes three elements: autonomy, mastery, and purpose. Autonomy has to do with the desire to direct our own lives. Mastery is our urge to get better and better at something that matters. And purpose is the yearning we have to do what we do in the service of something larger than ourselves.

EXHIBIT DESIRE

In my book *Marching Bands and Drumlines: Secrets of Success from the Best of the Best,* I interviewed Paul Rennick,

Percussion Instructor at the University of North Texas, about how he achieves excellence. He said desire was one of the primary factors he works on with his students. According to Rennick, "I work on their desire level pretty subconsciously. I get them to care about what they're doing as much as possible. And if they care about what they're doing, they will try harder. And if they try harder, they will probably play better. It's a snowball effect. What you'll find is that a lot of my groups are almost self-maintained. You'll hear corrections from people within the [drum] line in the same general positive way. When they care about it that much, they communicate that caring in their performance and it affects you."

Desire is also about passion. Without question, passion is one of the keys to success in any endeavor. When we are passionate about something, we are positive, hopeful, and energized. We are inflated rather than deflated. I have always believed that one of the best feelings in the world is the feeling of anticipation—having something to look forward to. It could be a vacation, a date, or a big performance or presentation. Or it could be waiting to hear if your book will be published, if you were accepted into college, or if you got the new job you applied for. This desire and passion for wanting to be successful is what hunger is all about, and this feeling of anticipation fills us with reservoirs of energy that helps us continue to work toward excellence.

NOT HUNGRY?

Do you find it difficult to be proactive, begin with the end in mind, become self-motivated, and exhibit desire? Do you find it challenging to take action and get yourself going? Do you struggle with knowing what you need to do and then doing it? Author and leadership expert John C. Maxwell offers this advice: "Act your way into feeling, rather than feel your way into acting." By taking positive action even when you don't feel like it, you will start to feel some momentum. You will start to feel hungry. When you decide to take that initiative, you will start to crave excellence and nothing less will satisfy you.

LESSONS ON EXCELLENCE—*HUNGER*

What makes NBA superstar Kobe Bryant one of the best players in the world? Is it his talent or his work ethic? Or could his talent be *the result* of his work ethic—his hunger—to be the best? According to pakistanbasketball.com, a site dedicated to pursuing excellence in basketball for the love of the sport, "You have numerous gifted athletes who make it to the NBA stage but after they make it, they just disappear. It's really up to them whether they have what it takes to remain, whether they have that eternal desire to be the best... and that's just what sets apart players like...Kobe."

Kobe's workout starts at 5:00 a.m. every day and comprises six days a week, six hours a day, and six months of training. This is how one of the best players in the game prepares to get to the pinnacle of his profession and stay there, and the results speak for themselves. Kobe Bryant knows what it takes, and in his own words, "You have to want it; you have to feel like you're about to cough up blood."

THE NEXT STEP —

1. Give three examples of intrinsic and extrinsic motivation in your life.
2. In what ways can you be more proactive, which would lead to better results in your work?
3. Do you believe that life happens to you, or that life is designed by you? Explain.
4. Describe one thing you are passionate about and look forward to achieving.

2

Effort

A guy who gives you less than what he has to give is, one, telling you what he thinks of you, and two, telling you what he thinks of himself.

Pete Carril, Hall of Fame basketball coach,
Princeton University and Sacramento Kings

You can look all you want, but you will not find any shortcuts to success. Legendary UCLA basketball coach John Wooden said, "There is no trick, no easy way. Success travels in the company of very hard work." As we saw in our first chapter, you must be hungry to achieve excellence. You must be proactive, begin with the end in mind, become self-motivated, and exhibit desire to achieve your goals. Once those skills start to become part of your make-up and mindset, you must develop a work ethic that is second to none. You must develop mental skills and an ability to concentrate and focus that sets you apart. And you must develop the competence and confidence to execute—to finish the job at a high level. These three qualities—hard work, focus, and execution all come together to define your effort.

HARD WORK

One of the most profound fundamentals of achieving success in life has always been—and always will be—hard work. The cliché "you get out of it what you put into it" is as true today as it was hundreds of years ago. Hard work is the price we all have to pay for success, and though success is never guaranteed, hard work puts you in the best position to achieve it. It is one of life's most important values and something we can apply to anything we want to accomplish. A strong work ethic is often instilled in us by our parents, mentors, and the goals we set for ourselves. Sometimes our work ethic is even ignited by wanting to prove others wrong and, at the same time, proving something to ourselves.

BACK HOME AGAIN IN INDIANA

After graduating from high school, I felt I was a good percussionist. I was active in the band and had competed in solo and ensemble festivals each year, winning blue ribbons and medals symbolizing outstanding achievement. I was enthusiastic about music, playing the drums, and being part of something bigger than myself. Pursuing my passion in college and majoring in music was my goal.

When I arrived at Ball State University as a freshman, I auditioned for the marching band and quickly discovered I was in the bottom tier of players. After not making snare drum, tenors, or bass drum, I ended up trying out for cymbals. Unfortunately, many percussionists tend to look down on playing cymbals in marching band and consider it a "dumping ground" for weak players and not nearly as "cool" or challenging as playing one of the drums. When I was offered a spot in the cymbal line, I was demoralized and ready to quit, until Dr. Joseph Scagnoli, Director of Bands at Ball State, asked me to give it a chance. Doc said he needed team players who would contribute and asked that I put the interests of the band ahead of my own. It was a life lesson I have never forgotten as I proudly played cymbals in the Ball State University "Pride of Mid-America" Marching Band that season. I became a better musician, made lifelong friends, and experienced one of the biggest turning points in my life in terms of learning what hard work was all about.

I decided to major in Music Education at Ball State and learned that my marching band experience was just the tip of the iceberg. My very first percussion lesson was with the late Richard Paul, formerly of the Indianapolis Symphony Orchestra and one of the percussion professors at Ball State. I remember sitting in his office talking about my musical experience in high school. After telling him I played the snare drum, I pointed to the marimba and said, "But I don't play *that*"–as if I didn't have to, as if it were optional. He made it very clear to me that if I wanted to pursue a degree in percussion, I would have to learn how to play the marimba.

It was apparent that I was significantly behind my peers. I had little talent and a weak musical background, and I had never studied with a private teacher on a regular basis. However, I soon discovered that what I did have was a work ethic that was second to none. I practiced an average of six hours a day my freshman year and presented a freshman recital that summer that included a marimba concerto. I played snare drum in marching band my sophomore, junior, and senior years and *taught* the Ball State Drumline my fifth year as an undergraduate. Part of teaching the drumline included building a culture where equality was valued and the cymbal line was respected. Years later, I wrote an article for the Percussive Arts Society journal *Percussive Notes* titled "Motivating the Marching Cymbal Line," which would help many marching bands and drumlines across the country become more cohesive as a team. If you would have told me then that I would one day become a tenured full professor at a major university and publish a book about marching band leadership, I would have thought you were crazy. Looking back, it was all due to hard work.

TWO OF THE BEST ON HARD WORK

John Wooden valued hard work so much as a coach and teacher that he made "industriousness" one of the cornerstones to his famous Pyramid of Success. Wooden biographer Steve Jamison states, "For most people, 'work' meant going through the motions, putting in time, enduring boredom. Industriousness, as [Coach] called it, meant true work at your highest capacity; fully engaged, totally focused, and completely absorbed. No clock-watching, no punching in and out, no going through the motions...In fact, industriousness entails rising above the level of hard work."

Mike Krzyzewski writes about effort in his book *Beyond Basketball:* "I want kids who hear that they are going to have to work hard and then get excited about how much they will improve as a result...Work is necessary if you want to improve. It is the road you have to follow to become better...It is no coincidence that my best players have been the hardest workers."

TALENT IS NOT ENOUGH

Several authors have written books about the talent myth, including John C. Maxwell's *Talent Is Never Enough,* Daniel Coyle's *The Talent Code,* and Geoffrey Colvin's *Talent Is Overrated.* These books—and others like them—profess that hard work is the key to attaining excellence, not talent. In Colvin's article "What It Takes to Be Great," research shows that the key to achieving greatness in any endeavor is not talent, but "painful and demanding practice and hard work." According to Colvin, "You will achieve greatness only through an enormous amount of hard work over many years...Talent has little to do with greatness. You can make yourself into any number of things, and you can even make yourself great."

The key to unlocking greatness, then, is deliberate, consistent effort. But where does this commitment to deliberate, consistent effort come from? According to Noel Tichy, business professor at the University of Michigan, the origin of effort can be traced back to the first value we discussed—hunger. "Some people are just more motivated than others," says Tichy, "and that's the existential question I cannot answer—why."

Personally, I believe effort comes from the realization that there really is no other way to achieve excellence. NBA player Mike Miller says simply, "How much work you put in is how successful you are going to be at the end." And Colvin states, "If great performance were easy, it wouldn't be rare...Maybe we can't expect most people to achieve greatness. It's just too demanding. But the striking, liberating news is that greatness isn't reserved for a preordained few. It is available to you and to everyone."

FOCUS

When people talk about hard work, they often refer to the physical effort—the training, practicing, conditioning, and "heavy lifting." But *mental* effort is just as critical to your success. Ask Olympic athletes about their preparation and you will hear about their rigorous physical *and* mental regimens. Renowned sports psychologist Gary Mack proclaimed, "Once you reach a certain level of competency, the mental skills become as important as the physical skills, if not more so."

Focus is a skill that must be continually developed to achieve excellence. Basketball legend Michael Jordan used to tell his teammates during practice to focus like a laser, not a flashlight. When I advise my percussion students on *how* to practice, I emphasize practicing with a high level of concentration, awareness, focus, intensity, intent, and purpose. When they focus, they are at their best. Their minds are engaged, in addition to their ears and hands. When they do not focus, they do not come close to performing to their potential. Although playing a musical instrument is often considered a physical, kinesthetic activity, excellence can only be obtained when mental effort is fully engaged. Musicians, as well as other high achievers, have to be aware, notice, and pay attention to what they are doing and stay in the moment to achieve peak performance.

There is a saying in competition: "You must be present to win." In this case, being present does not refer to being somewhere physically, but rather to keeping our minds in the present moment—in the *now*. One of the most effective mental skills we can develop for staying in the present moment and attaining peak performance is visualization.

VISUALIZATION

Visualization is the process of practicing your performance in your mind. According to Jon Gorrie, in his excellent book *Performing in the Zone,* "Visualization is a technique which can be employed to help 'program' your subconscious mind for success. When visualizing, you use your imagination to see, hear, feel, and fully experience the results you would like to achieve."

Try this exercise. Sit or lay down in a quiet place with no distractions. Relax, close your eyes, and visualize yourself giving a speech, presentation, or performance that you have coming up. Notice what you are wearing, what your surroundings look like, and your audience. See yourself giving the speech, presentation, or performance in real time, or imagine watching yourself as a member of the audience. Visualize it going extremely well, your ideal performance. Notice how you feel afterwards and the audience's response. Repeat this process several times before the actual event. By the time you get to the big day, your mind thinks you have already done it successfully several times. Your brain doesn't know the difference! According to Gorrie, "Sports scientists concluded that the subconscious mind cannot differentiate between what is real and what is imagined." If you can replicate the experience in your mind and visualize as many details as possible, you will be mentally prepared to be at your best when it counts.

According to golf legend Jack Nicklaus, his mental training was like "going to the movies." In their article "How the Mind Affects the Body," Gay Hendricks and Jon Carlson said, "[Nicklaus] imagines each shot from start to finish before he actually makes it—mentally setting up, swinging, hitting the ball, seeing it take off, land, and roll to a stop." According to Hendricks and Carlson, professional weightlifters "mentally picture their lift just before the actual attempt. When they stand in front of the bar and close their eyes, they are lifting it mentally." Skiers use visualization and mental rehearsals to review "every rise, hairpin, and dropoff on course, [so] on the day of the actual race there aren't any surprises."

Olympic gold medal swimmer Kieren Perkins credited his success in the 1992 and 1996 games to visualization. "I start months before the event. I just sit there and visualize the race in my mind. I dive into the pool. I'm swimming strongly. I'm out in front. The crowd [is] roaring, I can hear them. No one can catch me. I even see myself...with the gold medal placed around my neck."

Visualization works and is an excellent technique to sharpen and improve your focus. It takes some effort and a little time, but always has a huge payoff. If you want to work toward excellence, you have to do some mental work as well.

EXECUTION

Execution is the realization of effort. It is game day. It is the ability to knock down the free throws, kick the winning field goal, or sink the 10-foot putt. Execution is about coming through when it counts *as a result* of the hard work and focus you invested in your preparation. It is the *end* when you begin with the end in mind.

One of John Wooden's favorite maxims about execution was "don't mistake activity for achievement." Everybody's busy, and everyone's life is filled with lots of activity. This can sometimes mislead us into thinking we are working toward excellence. But time that is just filled up with busy activity does not necessarily translate into achievement. There are many busy people with a mediocre work ethic. There are many active people who lack focus. And there are many people who wake up early, go to work every day, and spin a dozen plates without really accomplishing very much.

Achievement is something different. Achievement is about what you are actually able to accomplish and produce. My friend and colleague Mike Sammons says, "You are judged by what you actually produce, not what you wanted to produce, what you said you would produce, or what you intended to produce." And author and speaker Brian Tracy put it this way: "Some people are simply not serious about success. They want to be successful, they imagine being successful, they wish they were successful—but they haven't taken the serious steps that are needed to achieve their dreams."

Achievement is about execution and getting things done. It is about consistently giving great effort and making the sacrifices necessary to succeed while not making any excuses. This is only possible if you have developed a strong work ethic and focus. Working toward excellence means exactly that. The hard work you put in toward your goal will, eventually and inevitably, lead you toward excellence—if you stick with it, believe in yourself, and refuse to settle for anything less.

SETTING GOALS

One of the best ways to focus as you work toward excellence is to constantly set goals. Brian Tracy said, "The ability to set goals and make plans for their accomplishment is the 'master skill' of success. It is the single most important skill that you can learn and perfect. Goal-setting will do more to help you achieve the things you want in life than will anything else you've been exposed to."

It is important to keep in mind that your effort toward execution is largely dependent on the goals you set. According to John Hamm in his book *Unusually Excellent,*

> Leading the goal-setting process to arrive at objectives that are perfectly sized is very tricky work... Goals that are clearly beyond any reasonable confidence of achievement are worse than easy goals—

they actually disengage the energy in the team...
Leaders need to learn the fine line between an
invigorating challenge and a wholly deflating expectation. They also need to realize that everyone
on the team may not share their level of maniacal
commitment...When dealing with high-perform-
ing types, you will need to resist their natural am-
bition to add value to the agreed-to set of goals by
wanting to commit to even bigger results. There
is already enough complexity in most ambitious
goals...The trick is to reframe success in terms of
mastering the fundamentals, producing results,
and learning more about the work along the way.

In the end, effort must lead to execution, and execution must lead to results. Hamm states, "At the end of
the day, leaders are held accountable; they get paid to
produce the agreed-upon results." What are the results of
your effort? Do you feel you have earned excellence based
on your hard work, focus, and execution?

LESSONS ON EXCELLENCE — *EFFORT*

Noted educator, clinician, and motivational speaker Dr.
Tim Lautzenheiser starts his leadership workshops by
asking the audience to raise their hands as high as they
can. They do. His next instruction is, "Now raise them
a little higher." Again, they do. After looking around the
room at hundreds of half-hearted efforts the first time,

Dr. Tim engages his followers by simply asking, "So why didn't you do that the first time?"

THE NEXT STEP —

1. Do you usually take your work as far as you can? Why or why not?
2. What motivates you to work hard?
3. How does/could visualization help put you in a position to succeed?
4. Do you sometimes mistake activity for achievement? How well do you execute?

AUGUSTA
NATIONAL GOLF CLUB

AUGUSTA NATIONAL is the home of The Masters, the first of four major tournaments on the PGA tour each year. Augusta is known for and defined by its standards of excellence—for the golf course, its members, and the PGA professionals who play on its historic landscape. The brand statement for The Masters is "A Tradition Unlike Any Other," which is upheld by the rich history of past champions, the aura and mystique of the course itself, and the incredibly high level of performance demanded from the best players in the world.

According to Ted Johnson's article "The Masters: 10 Things They Don't Tell You about Augusta National on TV," "No tournament has such allure, yet it is the only major played at the same course year in and year out. No course in major tournament use has Augusta National's contours, especially on the greens, and no course has a back nine that can induce such drama."

One example of the standards of excellence Augusta requires is the famous flora covering the golf course. "If an early spring comes, grounds crews will put ice under the azaleas to slow down their blossoming. They want everything in full color come Masters week." Another example is the dedication and commitment to uncommon resources

23

for course maintenance. "Get there early enough [and] you will find more than 60 people working on the course, mowing, raking, [and] edging....It's a standard that any other course cannot meet, much less your local muni [municipal course]. But then, there's no other course in the America that has the resources of Augusta National when it comes to maintenance."

In addition to keeping the course in pristine condition, the standards of excellence apply to people even more so than the course itself. According to one blogger, "All members of Augusta National, and the previous winners should lead a life beyond reproach. Their character should be in good standing and each should strive for excellence in their endeavors on and off the course...Augusta expects nothing more and nothing less."

3

Process

The fight was won long before I entered the ring.

Muhammad Ali, legendary champion boxer

Despite the importance of effort, our society tends to overvalue results and undervalue process—the very process that leads to the results we are aiming for. We value concerts over rehearsals, winning over practice, and grades over studying. Foolishly, we expect to succeed and achieve a desired result despite the process we use, as if it were optional. According to author Thomas Sterner, "We have a very unhealthy habit of making the *product*—our intended result—the goal, instead of the *process* of getting there. We look at the process...as almost a necessary nuisance we have to go through in order to get to our goal."

We expect the concert to go well, despite punctuality, attendance, and focus problems in rehearsal. We expect

25

to win the game, even though our practice habits fall short of what we are capable of. We expect to get an A on the test, even though we waited until the night before to study. Who do we think we are?

Duke University basketball coach Mike Krzyzewski said, "To have a championship season, you have to have championship practices." If we want to achieve excellence like Coach K, we should take his advice and come up with a game plan to have our own championship practices every day. Challenge yourself to come up with a championship process—and watch what happens.

IMPROVE YOUR STARTING POINT

Oklahoma basketball coach Lon Kruger focuses on the process of working toward excellence by improving his team's starting point. This is a simple way to evaluate the growth, improvement, and progress of an individual or team. According to Kruger, "We want our team to be better at the beginning of the next season than we were at the beginning of the last season. We work to have more talented players with better habits [and believe] teams must improve throughout the year...If we improve every day in practice that means we enter the next practice or the next game at an improved starting point every time... This philosophy brings results because it forces you to focus on improving just a little bit every single day." Kruger sums up his philosophy by saying, "We live in a fast-paced, results-oriented world. Because of this it can be difficult to lead. Improvement in an organization—or even an individual—does not happen overnight. It is a by-product of a process."

So teach your students, your players, and your employees to improve their starting point every day. If you always have to review everything and start over, you are basically treading water, running in place, and spinning your wheels. Improving your starting point requires *retention,* as excellence cannot be obtained by observing Groundhog Day week in and week out. Coach John Wooden put it this way:

> My performance ideal for the team was a gradual continuum of improvement—better and better, not up and down, one day good and the next day not so good. I sought slow, steady, sure improvement. It does not come all at once, but rather hour by hour, day by day. Ideally our team would play at its highest level in the last half of the last game of the season. That was my vision, my ideal. Each day some progress, always moving forward, teaching and learning, better and better, until finally the team performs at its full level of competency when it counts.

MICROWAVE OR CROCKPOT?

As previously mentioned, we live in a culture of instant gratification, a "microwave" society. We want results, and we want the rewards of those results now. We think excellence can occur quickly, but we know better. Excellence takes time. It cannot be texted, emailed, or found on Facebook. Working toward excellence is a process, just like writing a book, composing a piece of music, or crockpotting a meal. It takes time and patience. It takes staying in the moment, giving your mind time to think, being patient, and understanding that if you do that each day the results will take care of themselves.

Excellence must be crockpotted, not microwaved. Microwaving is fast, rushed, and does not taste very good. Crockpotting is slow and steady, and as the meal simmers over time, it is much more satisfying. If we want to achieve excellence, we have to crockpot the process.

THE PROCESS OF EXCELLENCE

While most high achievers agree that quality practice is more important than quantity (how *much* someone practices), excellence cannot occur without practicing for large amounts of time. According to Matthew Syed in his book *Bounce*, studies show that, though each individual is different, "A minimum of ten years [of practice] is required to reach world-class status in any complex task...Ten years, then, is the magic number for the attainment of excellence." Malcolm Gladwell in his book *Outliers* says, "Most top performers practice for around one thousand hours per year, so I re-describe the ten year rule as the ten-thousand hour rule. This is the minimum time necessary for the acquisition of expertise in any complex task."

According to Syed, a research study by Florida State University psychologist Anders Ericsson describes the importance of process to achieving excellence. "Violinists at the renowned Music Academy of West Berlin in Germany were divided into three groups. The first group comprised the outstanding students: the boys and girls expected to become international soloists, the pinnacle of musical performance...The second group of students was extremely good, but not as accomplished as the top performers. These students were expected to end up playing in the world's top orchestras, but not as star soloists. In the final group were the least able students: teenagers studying to become music teachers, a course with far less stringent admission standards." It was discovered that "by the age of twenty, the best violinists had practiced an average of ten thousand hours, *more than two thousand hours more than the good violinists and more than six thousand hours more than the violinists hoping to become music teachers.* The conclusion, according to Syed, was that "top performers had devoted thousands of additional hours to the task of becoming master performers... Purposeful practice was the only factor in distinguishing the best from the rest."

As we saw in our last chapter, and as Ericsson and his colleagues conclude, "A paradigm shift in the way excellence is understood [had occurred]—that it is practice, not talent, that ultimately matters," and that the key is "a lifelong persistence of deliberate effort to improve performance." Syed summarizes Ericsson's results on the value of process by stating, "When we witness extraordinary feats, we are witnessing the *end product of a process measured in years.* What is invisible to us—the submerged evidence, as it were—is the countless hours of practice that have gone into the making of a virtuoso performance: the relentless drills, the mastery of technique and form, the solitary concentration...What we do not see is what we might call the hidden logic of success."

BE A FLY ON THE WALL

Most of the time, the process is hidden from view. People are not clamoring to go behind the scenes and attend a rehearsal, practice, or meeting. We just want to see the finished product. It's too bad, really, because the keys to success are found in the process, not the product. We have it backwards. We want to eat the meal but have no interest in what is going on in the kitchen. But we should. We should stand in line to buy tickets to the kitchen, if only to be a fly on the wall. Think about it. Excellence is created slowly, one day at a time, behind closed doors, when no one is looking. It is happening gradually—even though we can't see it yet—*if* we treat the process with great care and respect. And if that process continues on the same trajectory, excellence will be the result. Do you know someone who is not successful? Look at his process. Do you know someone who produces mediocre work? Examine her process. The answers to excellence and mediocrity are found in the process—every time. The process is everything.

LESSONS ON EXCELLENCE — *PROCESS*

One day Pablo Picasso was walking in the market when a woman saw him and said, "Mr. Picasso, how are you?" He said, "Fine." She pulled out a piece of paper and a pencil and asked, "Mr. Picasso, can you do a little drawing?" He said, "Absolutely!" So he does this little drawing and hands it to the woman, and the woman looks at it and says, "This is amazing!" and she starts to walk away. Picasso responds, "Excuse me..." The woman says, "Yes?" Picasso says, "That will be one million dollars." She says, "A million dollars? Mr. Picasso, it took you thirty seconds to do that." He said, "Ah, my dear lady, it took me thirty years to be able to do that in thirty seconds."

THE NEXT STEP —

1. How much do you value the process compared to the result? Explain your philosophy.

2. Are you willing to commit to quantity and quality practice in order to achieve excellence?

3. Describe what your championship practices look like as you work toward excellence.

4. Devise a game plan for crockpotting your next big goal.

Quality

By the work, one knows the workman.

Jean de la Fontaine, seventeenth-century poet

What comes to mind when you think of Apple, Lexus, or Harvard? What about Southwest Airlines, the New York Yankees, or Disney World? How about Oprah Winfrey, Peyton Manning, or Louis Vuitton? I am hopeful that one thing that comes to mind is that they all have a reputation for *quality*. It is the goal of companies to make quality products, schools to provide quality education, leaders to provide quality experiences, restaurants to provide quality food and service, and artists to give quality performances. People around the world value quality, seek it out, and are happy to pay for it. We are also quite disappointed when we don't get it.

One of the most influential books on excellence I have read is *Becoming a Category of One: How Extraordinary Companies Transcend Commodities and Defy Comparison,* by Joe Calloway. The book is about what separates excellent companies from good ones and what makes the best of the best unique. Calloway begins by saying, "Don't strive to be a leader in your category. Create a different category, and be the only one in it. That's the idea behind *Becoming a Category of One."* He goes on to say this about excellence: "Perhaps the most surprising lesson of all is that quite ordinary people who simply do what other people are not willing to do achieve extraordinary success."

As important as quality is, business leaders are now saying it is becoming more of a given, rather than a competitive advantage. "Quality has become an expected factor because quality is everywhere," says Calloway. "Everybody brings a quality product or service to the marketplace. If they don't, they practically disappear overnight...It is the price of admission to the game...the playing field called quality has in fact become level."

A LACKLUSTER LUNCH

Despite this positive trend of quality being the rule rather than the exception, you do not have to look very far or go very long to find a lack of quality products, service, or people. While working on this book, my wife and I stopped for lunch at a popular restaurant known for its quality. Little did we know we were about to enter the eatery of mediocrity.

Standing in line looking over the large menu on the wall, we first became annoyed when I had to repeat my order several times to a disengaged employee. During this exchange, my wife paid for our meals and found a table. After the promised three-minute wait for my food turned into fifteen, I was asked to pay a second time because I had waited so long! I sat down with my wife, looked at my food, and took in the overall sloppy presentation and apathetic service. To say the restaurant fell short of our expectations would be an understatement. In fact, we were so dissatisfied we promised never to frequent the restaurant again.

Willa A. Foster wrote, "Quality is never an accident; it is always the result of high intention, sincere effort, intelligent direction, and skillful execution; it represents the wise choice of many alternatives." When we sign our name to something, when we put a stamp on our work, we communicate to people what we stand for and what we believe in.

In addition to a quality product or service, quality is a value we must develop within ourselves. If we are going to work toward excellence, quality must become a personal standard and expectation in our work and life. This personal standard encompasses three primary areas: our performance level, our confidence, and our professionalism.

PERFORMANCE LEVEL

Performance level is the true test of quality. Whether evaluating a product, service, or performance, quality is the bottom-line standard we all expect. We are attracted to quality, in part, because it represents a high performance level. Virtuoso musicians, superstar athletes, and state-of-the-art technology are just some examples of the kind of performance levels we are striving to emulate. When we witness an outstanding performance, we witness quality. But as we discussed in the last chapter, we can't forget how much thought, hard work, sacrifice, and commitment went into the realization of that quality performance. According to Doug Hirschhorn in *8 Ways to Great,* "A woman went up to the world-renowned violinist Isaac Stern after a concert and gushed, 'Oh, Mr. Stern, I'd give my life to be able to play the way you do!' To which Stern replied gravely, 'Madam, I have.'"

CONFIDENCE

Quality performances are confident performances. For example, a quality presentation, concert, or athletic performance all result from thorough preparation, a prerequisite for confidence. In fact, confidence is the result of many of the values we have discussed in this book, such as effort, hard work, execution, practice, success, and process.

Getting Over the Hump

To help my students attain confidence, quality, and excellence, I push them to "get over the hump" in terms of learning, memorizing, and performing their music. I use a visual analogy—a large hump or a small mountain—that they have to climb individually and as a group as we work toward excellence together. More than anything else, the hump represents their confidence level, and the only way to get over it is to *feel* confident based on the work they put in—their effort, their consistency, and their execution and success. Students always know when they get over the hump. I always know when it happens too. I can see it in the way they carry themselves, in their eyes, and in the way they play. They are lighter, more relaxed, and freer. They also look forward to coming to rehearsal more! They look forward to playing, feeding their confidence, and influencing their peers.

I also know when they have not gotten over the hump. They hesitate, make excuses, and simply lack confidence when they play. I always tell them, "You will sound how you look." If they look relaxed and confident, they will sound relaxed and confident, and if they look tense and hesitant, they will sound tense and hesitant. Getting over the hump is like climbing to the top of a mountain and then exhaling as you look down at the beauty of the landscape. It is a feeling of pride in a job well done. It is peace of mind—a feeling of confidence.

In music, one of the best ways to get over the hump is to schedule smaller performances during the preparation process that will help prepare the group for the big performance or goal. It is amazing to watch the confidence of a group go up *after* they have had their first performance! In other words, the first performance helps push them over the hump, and they come to the next rehearsal completely different players, more confident players. It is like a metamorphosis has occurred. They exude a "been there, done that" attitude, as if they have felt confident all along.

So to achieve quality and attain the confidence that will lead to excellence, encourage those you lead to get over the hump. Remember to visualize the hump as a small mountain or even a threshold that, once crossed, will allow your people to exhale and move closer to the quality they are striving for.

The Confidence Scale

Another technique I use to develop confidence in my students and bridge the gap between where they are and where they need to be is the *confidence scale.* The confidence scale is designed to signal whether a player is over the hump and in a position to succeed and have a quality performance. For example, I often ask, "On a scale from 1–10 (with 10 being the best), how confident are you on this piece?" In order to have a chance at achieving quality and excellence, one's confidence level, I believe, must be a 9 or 10. If students are a 7, then they immediately know they need to raise their score and close the gap if they are going to meet the quality standard. Students who do not practice and come to rehearsal unprepared usually rate themselves at a 5 or lower. With this low confidence level, they have no chance of being successful.

Without question, the key to confidence—and earning a 9 or 10 on the confidence scale—is *preparation*. Two of Coach John Wooden's favorite maxims that I have used often are "You have to earn the right to be confident" and "Failing to prepare is preparing to fail." And Louisville basketball coach Rick Pitino stated, "To achieve great things, you must deserve them." To achieve something of quality, you have to be confident.

PROFESSIONALISM

Architect Frank Lloyd Wright said, "A professional is one who does his best work when he feels the least like working." Professionalism refers to the three E's—expertise, ethics, and excellence—and is often measured by an individual's or organization's standards for producing quality work or services. Professionalism also means getting paid for what you do. According to tipsforsuccess.org, "Society does not emphasize the importance of professionalism, so people tend to believe that amateur work is normal. Many businesses accept less-than-good results."

And author and leadership expert John C. Maxwell often says, "People do not pay for average." Well, actually they do, but they are not happy about it afterwards!

As Director of the Clemson University Steel Band, I have a statement in my syllabus about quality, excellence, and professionalism.

Being a Professional

When you get paid to play music, you are considered a professional. When people hire us, they expect quality—period. There are no excuses. Not being prepared is simply not an option. For this reason, Gigging Steel Band is different from all other ensembles you have ever played in. One of our goals is to get hired again by the same people, because they know what they are getting with their money. Word of mouth spreads very fast as well. Remember—people don't pay for average. Would you pay for an average meal, an average movie, an average book, an average concert, an average cell phone, or an average computer? People pay for quality and excellence.

NBA Hall of Fame coach Chuck Daly said, "You get paid to play eighty-two nights a year," meaning professional basketball players have eighty-two games on the schedule and taking a night off—mentally or physically—is not an option. Daly commented, "It's very easy and tempting for a player to take some nights off, shift into cruise control, and be careless in his approach." According to his players, Coach Daly would not tolerate "mental vacations and was adamant [they] put out maximum effort every night." One player said, "Chuck taught us to be professional as players and people. Be ready to play every game—that's what you get paid for."

According to author Pat Williams' book about Chuck Daly titled *Daly Wisdom,* "Failure to perform at the highest level really is cheating. Players who allow themselves to become lazy are holding out on their employer, their teammates, and the ticket buying public." Williams asks, "Is your employer getting his money's worth from your daily performance? How about your co-workers and your family?" "Professionalism," says Daly, means "you've got to come prepared to play every day." Now that is what being a professional is all about.

A PHILOSOPHY OF QUALITY

Originally written in 1974, Robert Pirsig's *Zen and the Art of Motorcycle Maintenance* tells the story of the author's motorcycle trip from Minnesota to California with his son Chris. According to Wikipedia, "The book sold five million copies worldwide. It was originally rejected by 121 publishers, more than any other bestselling book, according to the *Guinness Book of Records.*" The trip, as well as Pirsig's personal approach to connecting with himself, his son, and his friends, includes several philosophical discussions called "Chautauquas" told throughout the journey. Many of these discussions focus on the subject of quality: what quality is and is not, and whether it can be defined.

One of the earliest examples of Pirsig's interest in quality happens at the beginning of the book when he takes his motorcycle into a shop for repair. Though he would eventually master the skills of motorcycle maintenance himself, he said, "It wasn't important enough at the time to justify getting into it myself, having to learn all the complicated details and maybe having to order parts and special tools...when I could get someone else to do it in less time." Leave it to the professionals, he figured. They were the expert mechanics. If for no other reason, he would have peace of mind as a result of their quality work.

What he experienced at the shop, however, was not quality work at all. According to Pirsig, when he entered the shop, "A radio was going full blast and they were clowning around and talking and seemed not to notice me. When one of them finally came over he barely listened to the piston..." They were indifferent. They didn't seem to care.

Two weeks later, the motorcycle malfunctioned again. "When I brought it back they accused me of not breaking it in properly." Fix it, charge for it, fix it again, then blame the customer? Not the standard of quality we have discussed so far in this chapter by any means. Pirsig even noticed the incompetence right in front of his eyes. "Just stop, I said politely, feeling like this was a bad dream. Just give me some new covers and I'll take it the way it is." The experience, though frustrating and unacceptable, caused Pirsig to become contemplative. He wanted to know how and why this could happen. As he explains:

The question *why* comes back again and again... Why did they butcher it so? They sat down to do a job and they performed it like chimpanzees. Nothing personal in it. There was no obvious reason for it. And I tried to think back into that shop, that nightmare place, to try to remember anything that could have been the cause.

The radio was a clue. You can't really think hard about what you're doing and listen to the radio at the same time. Maybe they didn't see their job as having anything to do with hard thought, just wrench twiddling. If you can twiddle wrenches while listening to the radio, that's more enjoyable.

Their speed was another clue. They were really slopping things around in a hurry and not looking where they slopped them...

But the biggest clue seemed to be their expressions. Good natured, friendly, easygoing—and uninvolved. They were like spectators. You had the feeling they just wandered in there themselves and somebody had handed them a wrench. There was no identification with the job. No saying, "I'm a mechanic." At 5 p.m. or whenever their eight hours were in, you knew they would cut it off and not have another thought about their work. They were already trying not to have any thoughts about their work *on* the job.

We can all relate to this story and have probably experienced something similar in a place of business. If you haven't, there's a good chance you will! We know what quality is in terms of service, a product, an experience, or even a person, but how do we define it? While Pirsig acknowledges quality exists, he says it cannot be defined. "Quality is a characteristic of thought and statement that is recognized by a non-thinking process. Because definitions are a product of rigid, formal thinking, quality cannot be defined."

A former rhetoric professor at a small college, Pirsig would emphasize "aspects of Quality such as unity, vividness, authority, economy, sensitivity, clarity, emphasis, flow, suspense, brilliance, precision, proportion, [and] depth..." Pirsig also reasoned that quality exists simply due to what the world would look like without it. "If you can't distinguish between bad and good in the arts they disappear," he said. "There's no point in hanging a painting on the wall when the bare wall looks just as good. There's no point to symphonies when scratches from the record or hum from the record player [in 1974] sound just as good...And interestingly, comedy would vanish too. No one would understand the jokes, since the difference between humor and no humor is pure Quality."

The question "What is quality?" both frustrated and fascinated Pirsig. In a simple exchange with a student who once asked him, "What do *you* think?" Pirsig replied, "I don't *know.*" "But what do you *think?*" the student insisted.

Some believe quality is subjective and lies in the eyes of the observer. "People differ about Quality," said Pirsig. "Not because Quality is different, but because people are different in terms of experience...A person who sees Quality and feels it as he works is a person who cares. A person who cares about what he sees and does is a person who's bound to have some characteristics of Quality...In arriving at the high-quality, beautiful way of doing it, both an ability to see what 'looks good' and an ability to understand the underlying methods to arrive at that 'good' are needed."

Well said, indeed. For without understanding the methods—the *process* of working toward excellence—real quality cannot be obtained.

LESSONS ON EXCELLENCE — *QUALITY*

There is an excellent company in the Pacific Northwest called Les Schwab Tires. They do what most everyone else does who sells tires— offer good, quality tires at competitive prices, a large selection, a written warranty, and good service. So what lifts Les Schwab to a level of excellence few in the industry have ever seen? They run to your car. Called "Sudden Service," this simple act of running to your car when you first pull up sends a powerful message of quality service. It is a message that says, "We want and appreciate your business. You have chosen to come here, and now it's our job to provide you with excellence. Let's get started!"

THE NEXT STEP —

1. Does your name stand for quality? Why or why not?
2. What steps can you take in your industry to become a Category of One?
3. Describe what it feels like to get over the hump as you work toward achieving quality.
4. Do you have a place like Les Schwab Tires where you live? If so, what is it about that place that keeps you coming back?

GOLF CLINIC AT SEA

GOLF HAS always been one of my passions and my main outlet for achieving balance in my life. I consider myself a serious golfer and was one of the top players on my high school golf team as a senior. When I am playing well, I shoot in the low 80s. I have broken 80 about a dozen times, with my best score being a 76. In fact, when I was playing and practicing a lot, I considered trying out for my college golf team and someday playing professionally, but based on how I was spending most of my time, I was more dedicated to music than I was to golf.

One of my early teachers and mentors was my cousin, Michael Balter, a professional percussionist and president of Mike Balter Mallets, one of the top percussion mallet manufacturers in the world. Michael once said to me, "Paul, you have to decide if you want to be Arnold Palmer or Buddy Rich." In the end, I chose to pursue a career in music and continue to play golf as a hobby that I really care about.

A few years ago, my wife April and I went on a cruise. We absolutely love to cruise—the traveling, the excursions, the scenery, and of course the food. It's the perfect getaway for us. In our cabin one night, lying next to the towel animal and cruise itinerary, was a sharp, full-colored flyer announcing a golf clinic with a PGA professional,

47

featuring the latest state-of-the-art technology on analyz-
ing your golf swing. The flyer read, "A virtual golf simulator
featuring V1 Pro analysis software enables the golf pro to
help you work on your swing while you are driving on
some of world's top golf courses." In essence, the simulator
records your swing by visually breaking it down, simulat-
ing a virtual golf course of your choice, and even compar-
ing your golf swing side by side with your favorite professional. This was an event I would definitely attend. I
highlighted the clinic in our itinerary and looked forward
to it with great anticipation. I even convinced April to go
with me! I figured there would be a lot of golfers on the
cruise, and seats might be hard to come by.

We arrived early and were guided to the clinic room,
careful to notice it was one of the lounges on board. "Inter-
esting place to have a golf clinic," I said to April. When we
took a seat, we soon discovered that the clinic was not at
all what we expected, and to say it was false advertising
would be an understatement. There was no virtual golf
simulator; no technology at all. There was just a man and
his 7 iron. In fact, the ceiling in the lounge was so low that
he couldn't even make a full swing. Everyone wanted to
escape.

The man introduced himself as a former pro on the
Champions Tour (formerly Senior PGA Tour) and wel-
comed us to the clinic. When we asked him about the
technology promised on the flyer, he pleaded ignorance.

Then, after noticing the dark ambience in the lounge, he asked us to move to the back where the lighting was better. Now we were trapped! We could not leave and had no choice but to sit through his clinic about how to swing a golf club with no technology, no lights, and no exit.

And no room to swing a golf club.

5

Consistency

Your only path to success is through a continuum of mundane, unsexy, unexciting, and sometimes difficult daily disciplines compounded over time.

Darren Hardy, publisher, *SUCCESS Magazine*

As we saw in our last chapter, quality has a huge impact on excellence. So does consistency. In fact, consistency is one of the invisible secrets to success. According to author and performance expert Joe Calloway, "The truth is that the most powerful tiebreaker is to simply do your job extremely well with every customer, every single time. Consistency of performance can be the most powerful differentiator of all. [People] aren't delivering really good service every time. It's just most of the time. Or, more likely, just some of the time. The great challenge for any company...is to deliver quality service consistently. And therein lies your potential differentiator–consistency."

OVERNIGHT SUCCESS

Entertainer Eddie Cantor said, "It took me twenty years to become an overnight success." To me, that pretty much sums it up. Whenever we hear of a new superstar exploding onto the scene, they seem like an overnight success. But if you carefully retrace their steps, their stories are the result of years of consistently doing the things necessary to succeed. What seems to happen suddenly is actually the result of a long process of consistency.

There is no substitute for consistency and no other value in this book that can compensate for it. Unless you live or work with a person who is consistent, it can be an invisible trait. Consistency is about slowly chipping away, making steady progress, and constantly getting better when others who are inconsistent are stagnating. Consistency is about having the self-discipline to value and embrace *repetition,* a key to learning, improvement, and achieving excellence.

BE LIKE MIKE

One of the qualities that made NBA legend Michael Jordan arguably the greatest basketball player of all time was his consistency. Not only did he play just as hard in practice as he did in games throughout his career, but he always gave his best effort regardless of the opponent. According to Bob Greene of the *Chicago Tribune,* "Mike play[ed] every game as if it were his last because he [knew] that in the stands [were] some fans who [would] never see him play again, other than that night." What an incredible approach and attitude to have! What if you were in a similar position to influence others by delivering the same kind of consistency as Michael Jordan? What would people say if they came to your workplace for a day and watched you do your job? Regardless of which day they visited, would they get your best? Would they be inspired on that day by watching you do what you do?

You see, unless you are Federal Express, success cannot be achieved overnight. Excellence is not a race to see who gets there the fastest. It is a goal that can only be reached—and sustained—by doing things well on a consistent basis, no matter how long it takes. Michael Jordan's consistency was most likely triggered when he was cut from his high school's varsity team as a sophomore. He said, "Whenever I was working out and got tired and figured I ought to stop, I'd close my eyes and see that list in the locker room without my name on it, and that usually got me going again." As they say, the rest is history.

A HAIL MARY

College professors can almost put money on the fact that at the end of every semester, there will be a few students who contact them after receiving their grades asking, "Is there anything else I can do?" Students often mention how much they *want* an A to improve their GPAs, or how much they *need* an A to stay in school or keep their scholarship. Like throwing a Hail Mary in football, this is a final, desperate attempt to try to make up for the lack of consistency the student displayed throughout the fifteen-week semester. "Is there anything else I can do?" My response to this question is usually, "You had four months to do something. Based on your work this semester, this is the grade you earned."

Our piano professor at Clemson University and dear friend Linda Li-Bleuel is a huge Green Bay Packers fan. When a student asks her, "Is there anything else I can do?" she turns to another football analogy, the last-second field goal. To paraphrase Linda, "Like in football, I tell students they can't expect to play poorly the entire game and kick a last-second field goal to make up for it. If they spent more time and effort being consistent throughout the season, it would not come down to the end."

THE JAPANESE STEAKHOUSE

Have you ever been to a Japanese steakhouse where they cook the food in front of you? Dinners traditionally come with soup, salad, shrimp appetizer, vegetables, rice, and your choice of chicken, steak, or seafood—and don't forget the ginger, mustard, and white sauce! The chefs are true virtuosos of their craft and are known for tossing their utensils in the air, twirling their salt and pepper mills, and engaging their customers with onion volcanoes, rice sculptures, and Taiko drumming on birthdays. Without question, the first time you visit one of these unique restaurants is a memorable experience, but after a while, you just want to go back for the food and can do without all the bells and whistles.

Next time you're dining in one of these restaurants, take a moment to look around the room. What you will see table after table, family after family, is chef after chef tossing, twirling, laughing, and drumming with happy customers. What you will observe night after night, week after week, and month after month is consistent entertainment and excellent food, whether you come at 4:30 for the early bird or 7:00 when you have to wait for a table. All restaurants are challenged every day to deliver consistency, as this keeps people coming back and is critical to an establishment's success. But at a Japanese steakhouse, we get to see the process up close. Remember in chapter 3 when I recommended we buy tickets to the kitchen so we can be a fly on the wall? Well, in this case, the kitchen comes to us. For a chef at a Japanese steakhouse, bringing your A game every night is what consistency is all about. It takes practice, creativity, and discipline, and the payoff is a reputation for excellence that people want to experience again and again.

THE COMPOUND EFFECT

In his book *The Compound Effect,* author and *SUCCESS Magazine* publisher Darren Hardy shares his operating system for success. Hardy says The Compound Effect is a simple system to follow, and that we have been "bamboozled for too long...There is no magic bullet, secret formula, or quick fix...We've lost sight of the simple yet proud fundamentals of what it takes to be successful."

What are these fundamentals? They are positive habits we choose to develop and apply to our lives consistently, which he believes is the ultimate key to success. By making small, smart choices and decisions consistently over time, this will result in a "radical difference." Hardy says, "Understanding The Compound Effect will rid you of [an] 'insta-results' expectation, the belief success should be as fast as your fast food, your one-hour glasses, your thirty-minute photo processing, your overnight mail, your microwave eggs, your instant hot water and text messaging." In short, The Compound Effect comes down to valuing the *process of consistency* and working toward excellence a little bit every day. "The Compound Effect is always working," says Hardy. "You can choose to make it work for you, or you can ignore it and experience the negative effects of this powerful principle."

WHAT CAN THE COMPOUND EFFECT DO FOR YOU?

Have you ever had to carry several heavy boxes into work when your parking lot is far away? What is your game plan? One strategy would be to drive your car up to the curb near the entrance, unload the boxes, drive back to the lot, park your car, walk to the boxes, and bring them in one or two at a time. Another strategy would be to put The Compound Effect into practice. When I recently encountered this situation, I decided it would be best to park my car in my normal lot and carry one box per day back to my office. After three days, all the boxes had been delivered and my trunk again had room for my golf clubs! By doing a little at a time—consistently—I got the job done. Sometimes in life, I think we try to carry too many heavy boxes with us all at once, which can lead to frustration, stress, and impatience—qualities that do not help us work toward excellence.

THE BACKPACK

A not-so-obvious example of The Compound Effect in action is the shaping of one's character. Many years ago, I attended a workshop on ethics. The speaker was average, dry, and curiously wore a backpack the entire time during his presentation. While he did not mention the backpack until the very end, we all speculated that perhaps he had a medical condition and had to carry a breathing machine of some sort, storing it in his backpack.

Time went by as he paced and communicated to the room, walking back and forth, all the while carrying a backpack that made him look a little ridiculous. With about five minutes remaining in this hour-long workshop on ethics, he paused and said, "I bet you are all wondering what's in the backpack and why I've been wearing it this whole time." He went on to explain that, "Bad decisions go in the backpack. They are heavy, especially the ones that only you know about. You have to carry them with you forever. The longer you carry them, the heavier the backpack gets. So, what is your goal? Keep the backpack light. Good decisions also go in the backpack, but don't weigh anything." And that is how the workshop ended.

Every decision we make in our lives shapes our character, one decision at a time. Coach John Wooden once said, "There is a choice you have to make in everything you do, so keep in mind that in the end, the choice you make, makes you." This is The Compound Effect in action.

LESSONS ON EXCELLENCE — *CONSISTENCY*

Former coach and current ESPN analyst Lou Holtz led the Notre Dame football team to nine bowl games and the 1988 National Championship during his tenure in South Bend, Indiana. During this period of college football excellence and unparalleled consistency, the Fighting Irish found themselves trailing at halftime one fall Saturday 20–0. The dejected players sat silently in their locker room waiting for their coach to address them. There they waited, wondering what he was going to say, what his message would be, and how upset he was. They waited. More time than usual passed. The players started to wonder if he was even coming at all. Then, after about fifteen minutes, the locker room door opened and Coach Holtz entered. "Oh, I'm sorry," he said. "I thought this was the *Notre Dame* locker room." Then he left, questioning their heart and challenging his team's identity. The team went on to win the game.

THE NEXT STEP —

1. Is your tiebreaker doing your job extremely well every single time, or are you still tied or even losing in this regard?

2. Give one example of applying The Compound Effect to your life. Perhaps you are training for a marathon, saving money for a new car, practicing for a recital, or carrying heavy boxes.

3. How heavy is your backpack? What decisions, if any, can you make to lighten the load?

4. How much do you value consistency in *your* locker room?

6

Leadership

You don't have to do things the way other people do. If you go out and do it a different way, you'll become a leader.

Tony Dungy, former Super Bowl–
winning football coach, Indianapolis Colts

One of the keys to reaching a high level of excellence is developing leadership skills that set you apart. Not only do you have to lead yourself by walking your talk, modeling self-discipline, and following through on your commitments, you must provide leadership to others if they are going to join you on the journey. In fact, excellence is rarely an individual accomplishment, but rather a team accomplishment and joint venture. In most cases, working toward excellence will require a group of people working together to accomplish a common goal.

FROM SUCCESS TO SIGNIFICANCE

Leadership expert John C. Maxwell said, "The bottom line in leadership isn't how far we advance ourselves, but how far we advance others." To me, this says it all. Some people who hold leadership positions believe leadership is just that—a position or title. Others believe leadership is all about the leader's accomplishments. What few leaders truly understand is that real, authentic leadership is not about you, but the people you are responsible for leading. So then, leadership is not really about *your* success at all, but the success of those under your supervision. Now read John C. Maxwell's quote again. If we want to work toward excellence, we have to provide others with excellent leadership.

YOUR LEADERSHIP SPOTLIGHT

As a college professor, my job performance is evaluated not only by my professional accomplishments, but by the quality of my leadership. The quality of my leadership is evaluated by my *students' performance.* In other words, if you want to see how effective I am as a teacher, come to any of my concerts and listen to my students perform. Their level of preparation and performance is the result of my teaching—for better or worse. Or better yet, come to any of my classes and observe my students, not me. Notice how engaged and focused they are and whether learning is taking place. Author Donald Phillips said,

"Who better to judge leadership qualities in a person than the people being led?" and former Secretary of State Colin Powell stated, "The performance of an organization is the ultimate measure of its leader." Too often, we have it backwards. In which direction does your leadership spotlight shine? Toward you, or toward your people?

In the college teaching profession, excellence is evaluated by the tenure and promotion process, a rigorous process examining one's teaching, research, creative activity, and service over the course of several years. Where some faculty get off track, I believe, lies in their *intentions* about tenure. Recently I was asked to contribute to an article titled "I've Been Hired as a College Percussion Instructor: What Now?" along with several of my esteemed colleagues. When asked the question, "What are some things instructors in their first few years of teaching should be doing to help aid in successfully achieving tenure when that time does arrive?" my response was based on the role leadership plays in achieving excellence:

> Don't think about it too much. Focus on your students, not on getting tenure. If you are doing things for the purpose of achieving tenure, your priorities will get out of whack. Our job as educators is to make a difference in the lives of our students, add value to them, and provide them with the best experience possible. If you show up for

work each day with this motivation, tenure will be a natural end result. This is an uncommon mindset, but one that is based on excellent leadership and intrinsic motivation. That said, you still have to embrace the tenure process, develop positive relationships with your colleagues, and build an excellent program and record of teaching, creative activity, and scholarship.

As an educator, I passionately believe that teaching and leadership are one in the same, and to become a better teacher, one must become a better leader. Look at any business, organization, school, or sports team, and you will discover that performance level is a direct reflection of the quality of leadership.

Too often, new technology and innovations claim to have improved teaching to the point of inferring that what has come before is no longer (or was never) good enough. Former basketball coach Swen Nater has notably stated, "Whenever some 'new' kind of teaching is tried, the point is that students learn more. The moment the focus shifts from what students are learning is the moment teachers risk getting off track. The end is student learning; the means is teaching. One does not become a better teacher just by adopting an approach that is in fashion or recommended. Teachers are more effective when their students learn more."

HAIL THE ZEN MASTER

It has been well-documented that basketball legend Michael Jordan did not win his first NBA championship with the Chicago Bulls until Phil Jackson became head coach. One of the turning points was when Jackson, known as "the Zen Master" for teaching his players Zen Buddhist philosophies of teamwork and harmony, implemented the famed triangle offense and convinced MJ to trust his teammates and make them better. No matter how great Jordan was individually, he could not achieve excellence alone in a team sport. He needed others, and it took the leadership of his coach to help him. Jackson did the same thing with Kobe Bryant and the Los Angeles Lakers, amassing an unbelievable total of eleven NBA championships by the time he retired.

John C. Maxwell has stated, "People say 'it's lonely at the top,' but that's not true. If you're up at the top all alone, nobody's following you. It's not lonely at the top. What real leaders do is they get off of 'the top.' They go to where the people are. Then they bring the people to the top with them."

If the top is excellence, then odds are there is a leader who has brought you to the top with them, or at the very least, has pushed you from behind. We all need leaders who have been where we want to go, who believe in us more than we believe in ourselves, and who want us to succeed. Those of us who are blessed to have those people in our lives often want to give back to them by working toward excellence and making them proud, carrying the torch, and continuing their legacy.

THE SUCCESS TRIFECTA

Each semester students often request to interview me about my career path. Towards the end of the interview, they usually ask me a question along the lines of "What is your advice on how to achieve success?" My advice always consists of three things: find your passion, build relationships with people, and become a lifelong learner of leadership.

FIND YOUR PASSION

You cannot work toward excellence if you are not passionate about what you do. You have to love it, look forward to it, and truly be enthusiastic about it. I always encourage my students to find their niche, and with that, their passion. Too many people in this world have jobs they do not enjoy, and even worse, feel stuck and do nothing to change their situation. They stay with their job to pay the bills, but lack the passion necessary to achieve excellence. One of the reasons excellence is rare, I think, is because those that achieve it truly have found their calling. They have found their passion. When you can find what you are meant to do on this earth, something that lights a fire within you, and something that motivates you every day, you have a chance to do something special. You have a chance to achieve excellence. Sports leadership expert Jeff Janssen asks, "Are you here for something to do, or are you here to *do* something?" Without question, those who are here to *do* something have found their passion and are working toward excellence. And they will achieve it.

BUILD RELATIONSHIPS WITH PEOPLE

The second piece of advice I offer is to constantly build relationships with people. Nothing is more important to your success than the relationships you form with others. The best way to build relationships is to put others first. Listen to them. Treat them with respect. Call them by name. Take a genuine interest in them. Take the initiative to call them, email them, and reach out to them. Show that you care. Be kind. And don't expect anything in return.

We talked at the beginning of this chapter about the fact that excellence is rarely an individual accomplishment, but rather a team accomplishment that usually requires a group of people working together to accomplish a common goal. Look at any excellent performance and you can be sure there is a team of people that helped make it happen. Leaders of a team, business, organization, or classroom must have the ability to build relationships with people if excellence is to be achieved. Excellence is too big a goal for one person. As John C. Maxwell said, "If you think you're leading and no one is following you, then you're only taking a walk." Build relationships with people, nurture them, and watch your success start to take off—as well as theirs!

BECOME A LIFELONG LEARNER OF LEADERSHIP

The last piece of advice I have is to become a lifelong learner of leadership. I believe that if you study leadership as well as the qualities of great leaders, these ideas will transfer to your own success. Warren Bennis said, "Excellence is a better teacher than mediocrity. The lessons of the ordinary are everywhere. Truly profound and original insights are to be found only in studying the exemplary."

I have a leadership library of over 150 books on the subjects of leadership, teamwork, success, coaching, and excellence. Many of my books are listed in this bibliography and feature world-class business leaders such as Jim Collins, John C. Maxwell, Pat Williams, Joe Calloway, Tony Hsieh, Stephen Covey, Jack Canfield, Darren Hardy, and John Hamm, as well as legendary sports leaders such as John Wooden, Phil Jackson, Mike Krzyzewski, Jim Calhoun, Michael Jordan, Vince Lombardi, Bill Walsh, Tony Dungy, and Bo Schembechler.

There are as many leadership styles as there are leaders, and I am always curious to find out what someone new has to say about the subject of leadership. One thing I have learned is that the more things change, the more

things stay the same. Excellent leadership is truly something you can hang your hat on, no matter when you
decide to get started. In the introduction to his revised
and updated book, *The 21 Irrefutable Laws of Leadership*,
John C. Maxwell states, "It's still true that leadership
is leadership, no matter where you go or what you do.
Times change. Technology marches forward. Cultures
differ from place to place. But the principles of leadership are constant—whether you're looking at the citizens
of ancient Greece, the Hebrews in the Old Testament, the
armies of the modern world, the leaders in the international community, the pastors in local churches, or the
businesspeople of today's global economy. Leadership
principles are unchanging and stand the test of time." My
leadership library has been invaluable to my own growth
and development as a leader and has provided me with
resources and inspiration to motivate others with quotes,
stories, and real-life examples that they can apply to their
own leadership journey.

THE 7 CS OF LEADERSHIP

Those that achieve excellence are leaders. There are
many books containing lists of qualities that excellent
leaders possess, from John C. Maxwell's *21 Indispensible
Qualities of a Leader,* to Pat Williams' *Seven Sides of Leadership,* to Jeff Janssen's and Greg Dale's *Seven Secrets of
Successful Coaches.* Of all the lists in my library, I have
used Janssen's and Dale's list the most when doing

leadership workshops. Since all leadership qualities are universal and not discipline-specific, and because these seven qualities all begin with the letter C and are easy to remember, I have renamed Janssen's and Dale's list "The 7 Cs of Leadership," adapted with permission from *The Seven Secrets of Successful Coaches* by Jeff Janssen and Greg Dale. If you want to improve your leadership skills as you work toward excellence, simply improve each one of the 7 Cs.

1. **Character.** Leaders are people of character and integrity who do the right thing. They are honest, trustworthy, and have the highest ethical standards. We looked at character in chapter 5 on consistency when we learned about the backpack. Remember, we all carry an invisible backpack around with us representing our character.

2. **Competence.** Leaders are competent, which means they "know their stuff." They have a thorough and comprehensive understanding of their game. Competence is knowledge and expertise that earns the trust and respect of others and gets them to follow you—both at first and over time. In the end, competence is a set of skills demonstrated by successful execution.

3. **Commitment.** Leaders are committed to excellence. Before they ask others to make a commitment, they lead by example. Commitment means

staying the course, following through, and persevering through adversity. Leaders show their commitment through their energy, resiliency, and passion and do not stop until they achieve their goal.

4.   **Caring.** Leaders are caring human beings. Earlier in this chapter, we looked at the importance of building relationships for your leadership success. To achieve excellence as a leader, you must care about your people and this caring must be authentic. Many great leaders agree that people don't care how much you know until they know how much you care.

5.   **Confidence.** Leaders are confident. In chapter 4 on quality, we took a hard look at confidence by examining how to get people over the hump and using the confidence scale. The hump is a critical place for any leader, as it often represents a turning point for a group's success. The confidence scale is not only a tool to evaluate your people, it can be a leader's compass on the road to greatness.

6.   **Communication.** Leaders are excellent communicators. They are good listeners as well as accessible and approachable. Leaders are open, transparent, and direct when speaking individually or collectively with their people and always strive to make communication timely and relevant. Lead-

ers know that the way they communicate is a key to their success.

7. **Consistency.** Leaders are consistent, which is not only one of the 7 Cs of Leadership, but one of the eight values for achieving uncommon success in work and life discussed in this book. Being consistent as a leader gives your people security in knowing what they can expect from you. This level of trust is important to them and helps create a culture of high performance.

Leaders are people who display and constantly work to improve the 7 Cs. They are people with goals, a game plan for achieving them, and a team to help them get there. Leaders are people with high expectations and standards and are not satisfied with the status quo. They are the ones we should all look to if we want to work toward excellence—because they have done it, are doing it now, and will continue to do it in the future. Become a lifelong learner of leadership and let these leaders mentor you like they have mentored me. It will be one of the greatest investments you will ever make.

LESSONS ON EXCELLENCE — *LEADERSHIP*

Early one morning at A.B. Combs Elementary School in Raleigh, North Carolina, the choir director called the school to say she was running late for her first period choir rehearsal. Her principal agreed to cover for her until she arrived and started heading towards her classroom. Before entering, the principal peeked through the door's window and noticed one of the fourth-grade students conducting and leading the group in warm-ups. When she opened the door to see which one of her teachers helped get the class organized, she saw no adults at all.

THE NEXT STEP —

1. Do you believe that leadership is not really about your success at all, but the success of those under your supervision?

2. If the performance of an organization is the ultimate measure of its leader, how is your organization doing these days?

3. Are you lonely at the top? Why or why not?

4. Have you found your passion? How well do you build relationships with people? Are you a life-long learner of leadership?

WYNTON MARSALIS

WYNTON MARSALIS is an internationally acclaimed musician, composer, band leader, educator, communicator, and ambassador of jazz. Originally from New Orleans, Wynton is the son of legendary jazz pianist Ellis Marsalis, who taught him the values of discipline, hard work, and respect. Now a giant among jazz trumpet players, Wynton grew up in a musical household with brothers Branford (saxophone), Delfeayo (trombone), and Jason (drums). Today, Wynton is the leader of the Jazz at Lincoln Center Orchestra, regarded by many as the finest big band in the world. Paying tribute to the jazz masters of the past while exploring the creativity and innovation of tomorrow, the orchestra influences generations of listeners with their music and their message.

In addition to setting the highest standards of performance, the orchestra's mission goes far beyond playing great music well. According to their website, "Jazz at Lincoln Center is dedicated to inspiring and growing audiences for jazz. With the world-renowned Jazz at Lincoln Center Orchestra and a comprehensive array of guest artists, Jazz at Lincoln Center advances a unique vision for the continued development of the art of jazz by producing a year-round schedule of performance, education, and broadcast events for audiences of all ages."

Early in his career, Marsalis was motivated by wondering if he would ever be good enough to make it. Even today, at the top of his profession, he displays a high level of emotional intelligence. When asked how his playing has changed in the last fifteen years, he humbly said, "I think [it is] the natural wisdom that comes with age. I also think I have a different type of weight in my sound and just [over] the fifteen years I know more music. So when I'm playing I think it reflects a deeper knowledge. I hear better too."

Marsalis is known as much for his dynamic communication skills as he is for his virtuosic musicianship. According to business leader Keith Reinhard, "Of all the motivational speakers we have ever invited to our worldwide management conferences, the visit by Wynton Marsalis is the one that stands out from the rest. Wynton inspired us with his remarkable insights into creativity, leadership, and excellence. His time with us made us a better, more creative company."

On stage, Wynton and his fellow ensemble members earn similar acclaim. According to a writer for *The Savannah Morning News*, "Sitting in the same auditorium with the well-known Wynton Marsalis was a privilege. Listening to music stirs the emotions; watching it performed motivates one for excellence. This is why I have made the journey. There is something gained in seeing the excellence of perfected craft; the delight in the faces of those who perform so well—the work of their hands filling a room with energy and enjoyment. I am motivated to perfect my life and skills, to create more excellence."

Marsalis' true legacy, however, may be as one of music education's biggest advocates. "Support of the arts," he says, "is a gift to our country." He believes jazz and music in general improves human relationships, brings people together, and keeps spirits alive. "Maybe the preoccupation with technological progress has overshadowed our concern with human progress," he remarked.

In his book *Moving to Higher Ground*, Marsalis states, "I hope to reach a new audience with the positive message of America's greatest music, to show how great musicians demonstrate on the bandstand a mutual respect and trust that can alter your outlook on the world and enrich every aspect of your life—from individual creativity and personal relationships to conducting business and understanding what it means to be American in the most modern sense."

Through his horn, his voice, and his conviction, Wynton Marsalis continues to create and inspire excellence for all who want to listen.

7

Time

Pay now, play later. Play now, pay later.

John C. Maxwell, leadership expert, author,
and speaker

T his quote from John C. Maxwell is about valuing time. In essence, he is saying that if we give our best effort from the very beginning of an endeavor, we will be so prepared by the end that we will be able to take our foot off the gas and relax a little, having put ourselves in a position to succeed. However, if we procrastinate and lack the self-discipline to get started, we end up wasting time and causing ourselves a great deal of stress, making it almost impossible—or at the very least much more difficult—to achieve excellence.

Coach John Wooden understood the value of time. "Don't think you can make up for it by working twice as hard tomorrow," he would say to his players. "If you have it within your power to work twice as hard, I want you to do it right now." Wooden also reflected on how time gave his team an edge. "Gradually, I had learned how to get the most out of a minute. In return, each minute gave back the most to our team. I valued [time], gave it respect, and tried to make each minute a masterpiece."

Wooden biographer Steve Jamison said, "Time, used correctly, is perhaps your most important asset. Wasting a single moment became painful for [Coach], like throwing a gold coin into the ocean never to be recovered." To this end, Coach Wooden also insisted on punctuality, but what made him uncommon was his belief that being late not only showed disrespect for others, but disrespect for *time!*

One of the great equalizers in this world is that everyone has twenty-four hours in a day. How we use those hours is what separates excellence from mediocrity. "Treat time carelessly and it will do the same to you and your organization," said Steve Jamison.

Most people waste time rather than value time. In my profession, when I tell my students our concert is in two months, they usually say to themselves, "Two months is plenty of time. No problem. I'm not too worried about it." In contrast, I say to myself, "We *only* have two months to reach the level of excellence that we expect. That's going to be a challenge." As the leader, I look at the big picture, counting down the months, weeks, and days of rehearsal as the concert approaches. Students, on the other hand, tend to experience a sense of urgency when they realize there is not nearly as much time as they originally thought. "The concert snuck up on me," one said to my dismay. "How is that possible?" I asked.

Without question, time is a value that deserves our attention as much as anything else we have talked about in this book. It relates directly to The Compound Effect and how long excellence really takes to achieve.

DON'T BE AFRAID TO SAY NO

I have always felt that "no" is a perfectly good answer. I also believe that if you make a commitment to everything, you are making a commitment to nothing. If excellence is your goal, it is important to value your time and have priorities. There is just no rhyme or reason to juggle a dozen balls or spin a dozen plates and have them all come crashing down.

Darren Hardy said, "[I used to be] a mile wide and an inch deep, and that's not how you strike oil!" Time is our most precious resource. If we say yes to everything, we become "a mile wide" and are spread too thin. We have too many irons in the fire, and nothing gets done at a high level of excellence. How could it? There is just not enough time to do that many things well on a consistent basis. Author David Heinemeier Hansson commented, "If you say yes to everything, everything you do won't and can't be great, and greatness is what the marketplace wants." In contrast, if we say no to some things along the way, we can start weeding out what is not important.

Saying no is never personal. Author Pat Williams put it this way: "You have a right to say no, period. You don't have to make up a lie. You don't have to justify yourself. You have a right to invest your time in any way you choose without explaining yourself to anyone. So cultivate the time-management skill of saying no."

If saying no makes you uncomfortable, you just have to work on getting comfortable with being uncomfortable. For example, I sometimes have to say no to my students. They may not like my decision in the moment, but they respect it and move on. Sometimes when their hunger, effort, or process is not what it should be, or if we just don't have enough time to prepare, I may have to make a decision to cut a piece of music they have been working on from our concert program. Remember, excellence takes time, and our goal is to crockpot our preparation, not microwave it. When this situation occurs, I usually explain to them that "no one cares what we *don't* play." In other words, in my opinion, it is better *not* to do something at all than it is to do it poorly. More often than not, biting off more than you can chew will lead to mediocrity.

Instead, eliminate the stress. Allow more time to focus on other things. The result is doing *less–better*. Less is more. By saying no, you are saying yes to doing less better and greatly improving your chances of achieving excellence. Rather than being a mile wide, we become narrow—more focused—and the quality of what we present to the world goes much deeper and offers more substance, confidence, and pride.

Business millionaire Warren Buffett says this is the key to his success: "For every one hundred great opportunities that are brought to me, I say no ninety-nine times." And the late Apple CEO Steve Jobs stated, "I am as proud of what we don't do as I am of what we do."

Make no mistake. Every minute counts and will add up in the end. Value and protect your time. Value and protect others' time. It will make all the difference in the world.

IT'S ABOUT TIME

Though it is said that some people do their best work when they don't quite have enough time, there are some things you can do to improve this value as you work toward excellence.

1. **Wake up earlier.** According to radio host and author Mel Robbins, "When it comes to being a master of your life, you are *never* going to feel like doing what you need to do. That's the skill you need to master: taking radical action. Life is the same as lying in bed; it's easier to hit the snooze and put things off. Whenever I get that hit-the-snooze feeling, I do the opposite. I push through the excuses and put my feet on the floor."

2. **Be punctual.** Being early is a habit, just like being late. A culture of excellence always includes punctuality and a culture of mediocrity always includes tardiness. Don't be the person running through the airport trying to catch your flight. Instead, be the person who unlocks the building.

3. **Get a planner.** According to the first page of the *At-A-Glance Quick Notes Monthly Planner,* "Thank you for choosing this...planning product to help you manage today's most precious commodity— your time. Although we can't put more hours in the day or days in the week, we are committed to developing products that keep you organized and make you more productive."

4. **Value every minute.** Don't waste time. Avoid people, tasks, and situations that do not move you in the direction of excellence. Remember that "no" is a perfectly good answer.

5. **Start and end on time.** Ending on time is just as important to people as starting on time, maybe even more so. Nothing is more frustrating to high achievers who plan than not knowing how long a meeting will last, or worse, going over the scheduled time because people were unorganized or unprepared. It is the leader's job to lead by example in this regard. When meetings, rehearsals, and practices start and end on time *consistently,* your people will be able to trust, count

on, and depend on you, which will lead to better morale and a higher likelihood of them working toward excellence.

6. **Mind the clock.** For people who mind the clock, 9:00 means 9:00, not 9:05 or even 9:01. It is similar to having a tee time at a golf course where things run like "clockwork." Several years ago, I did a clinic at Florida State University that was scheduled for 7:00 a.m. It was so early because this was the only common time the students were available for their studio master class. I arrived at 6:15 to set up, warm up, and become familiar with the instruments. Between 6:45–6:59 a.m., students arrived. Precisely at 7:00, Florida State percussion professor John Parks locked the door, introduced me, and I went on to give my clinic.

LESSONS ON EXCELLENCE — *TIME*

There is a saying in the Clemson Tiger Band: "To be early is to be on time, to be on time is to be late, and to be late is to be left behind." Many years ago, one of the band members missed the bus when our marching band departed on an away trip to Florida State. The rule was that if you missed the bus, it was your responsibility to arrange your own transportation. Realizing the error of his ways, the band member got in his car and started making the nine-hour drive toward Tallahassee. After some time passed, he noticed he needed to stop for gas but had no money. What he did have, however, were his golf clubs in the trunk. After exiting the interstate and finding a gas station, he went inside and offered his golf clubs as collateral, promising he would pay for the gas on the way back home from the game. The gas station attendant agreed and the band member made it to Florida, rejoining the band on the trip.

THE NEXT STEP —

1. How well do you value time? Do you make every minute count?

2. What ways can you improve punctuality in yourself and others?

3. Comment on this statement: "We cannot put more time into our life, but we can put more life into our time."

4. Do you tend to pay now and play later, or do you play now and pay later?

8

Perseverance

Don't stop believin'.

Journey, rock band

Perseverance is the ability to keep going during tough times, overcome adversity, and never give up. Perseverance is persistence plus resiliency, and it reveals our true character by causing us to look in the mirror, dig deep, and take responsibility for what will happen next. Perseverance is the inner strength you must have to succeed. If you were to study the careers and experiences of all the successful people in this book, you would find a time when they arrived at a crossroads and had to decide whether to give up or whether to persevere.

Successful people learn to *expect* adversity as they work toward excellence. They are not surprised when it comes and do not let it deter them from their goals. They adopt the attitude that adversity is part of the game, so bring it on! Understanding and accepting this reality at the beginning of your endeavor will help you be prepared and stay positive.

Things that are easy are not worthwhile. When we are not stretched, we do not grow. Perseverance is like a muscle. The more we exercise it, the stronger it becomes. Having the ability to persist and continue when things are not going well is often what separates the ordinary from the extraordinary.

BEAR DOWN

At the end of the day, we are all products of our experiences, both positive and negative. But perseverance is about how we *respond* to those experiences and how we handle success and failure. We can all understand the value of bouncing back from failure, but why do we need to persevere after achieving success? According to John C. Maxwell, today's success can be a "leadership landmine" if we become complacent. "Life is not a snapshot," says Maxwell. "You can't take a picture when you are at the pinnacle of your success and say nothing will ever change...The ability to let go of your successes and failures is absolutely essential."

Most of us will agree that we tend to learn more from failure than we do from success. Why? For one, failure gets our attention because we take it personally. Failure can cause us to become depressed and doubt our ability, lose confidence, and question whether our goals and dreams can ever be achieved. But people who know how to persevere use failure as fuel and motivation. It causes them to take stock of where they are and nudges them toward making changes that will lead to a different result the next time. In short, they become more determined. People who have not developed the muscle of perseverance usually quit, convincing themselves they are not capable of achieving their goals or, worse, blaming others for their circumstances. Dennis Coates and Meredith Bell, authors of *Strong for Leadership*, said of perseverance, "Just decide that after most people have dropped out, you'll be one of those still in the game."

Perseverance is a mental skill. It is the ability to trust, believe, and stay positive and optimistic when you see evidence to the contrary. It is about bearing down, pushing through, and being disciplined to never give up, no matter what challenges lie ahead.

DON'T GIVE UP, DON'T EVER GIVE UP

One of the most inspirational stories of perseverance I grew up with was that of the late North Carolina State basketball coach, Jim Valvano. His quote "Don't give up, don't ever give up" has resonated with sports fans for over two decades.

"Jimmy V," as he was known to those closest to him, was diagnosed with cancer in 1992, nine years after one of the greatest upsets in college basketball championship history. His 1983 N.C. State Wolfpack beat the highly favored Houston Cougars, who had future NBA Hall of Famers Hakeem Olajuwon and Clyde Drexler leading the way. N.C. State miraculously won 54–52 on a last-second dunk, coming off a thirty-foot prayer that turned out to be an air ball. After the horn sounded, Jimmy V was seen frantically running around the court looking for someone to hug. He was elated, basking in the opportunity to watch his players relish the moment. It was a storybook ending to a dream season that ended with David beating Goliath. For many coaches, this was the kind of moment that would define them.

A BIGGER MOMENT

It would turn out that Coach Valvano's true defining moment would come ten years later on March 4, 1993 at the ESPYs, the ESPN awards show that stands for "Excellence in Sports Performance Yearly." Jim Valvano was the first recipient of the Arthur Ashe Courage and Humanitarian Award at the first ESPY ceremony. According to Justin and Robyn Spizman in *Don't Give Up...Don't Ever Give Up,* "Jim's cancer was extremely difficult to fight. Doctors told him he had only a short time to live, and on the night of the speech, Jim was covered in tumors and could hardly muster the strength to make it to the stage to accept his award...he was in unbearable amounts of pain..."

But Jimmy V persevered. He summoned the strength to walk on stage and deliver a speech that would touch the lives of all those in attendance and millions of others watching on TV. Make no mistake. Jimmy V was in charge of that room. He connected with every person who listened, and despite his heartbreaking and painful ordeal, his message was uplifting, inspiring, and transcendent. He had hope. He was optimistic. He was grateful, humble, emotional, and honest. And because his words were so transparent and came from the heart, "the speech" became his legacy. While it is still accessible on YouTube and DVD, I thought I would share my favorite moments from Jimmy V's speech with you.

Time is very precious to me...Hopefully, at the end [of this speech], I will have said something that will be important to other people too.

To me, there are three things we should all do every day...Number one is laugh. You should laugh every day. Number two is think. You should spend some time in thought. Number three is you should have your emotions moved to tears...If you laugh, you think, and you cry, that's a full day. That's a heck of a day. You do that seven days a week, you're going to have something special.

Cancer can take away all of my physical abilities. It cannot touch my mind, it cannot touch my heart, and it cannot touch my soul. And those three things are going to carry on forever.

While certainly not all situations in life require this level of courage and perseverance, there are many lessons we can take from Jimmy V as we work toward excellence. Work hard; put your heart and soul into achieving your dreams; believe anything is possible; shine the leadership spotlight on others; be humble and positive; laugh, think, and cry every day; live life to its fullest; and most of all, don't give up, don't ever give up!

CLOSE TO HOME

We all have people in our lives who are pillars of courage and perseverance, people who face enormous challenges with incredible determination, spirit, and resolve. I would like to pay tribute to one such person in my family by sharing her story.

Kris Buyer is my stepmother, but she has always been more like a big sister since she married my dad. Richard, my father, is a physician—an internist for over forty years. Kris worked as a nurse, and when my sister Kennedy was born, decided to stay home and raise her. Even though I earned my doctorate, I broke the chain of physicians in my family, as my grandfather Morris—my dad's dad—was also a doctor. I have been around medicine much of my life and, though I am not fluent in the terminology, have always been aware of how skilled and knowledgeable a physician my father is.

In 2009, Kris, who was only forty-four at the time, was diagnosed with an extremely rare virus called the JC virus. According to Wikipedia, "The virus is very common in the general population, infecting 70 to 90 percent of humans." Most of us are exposed to the JC virus as children, but it usually remains latent in people with normal immune systems. However, for those with weaker immune systems like Kris, the virus can reactivate later in life and prove fatal with no known cure.

Upon diagnosis, Kris' condition was declining. The virus invaded her brain and started to affect her fine and gross motor skills, balance, and speech. My dad and Kris sought out experts throughout the country with little success. Doctor after doctor, no one knew how to fight this particular virus. They decided to try an unprecedented procedure to kill the virus and save Kris' life. Kris would undergo three white blood cell transfusions from her sister Lisa, injecting healthy white blood cells into her body in order to attack the virus. This was done along with boosting her immunity with daily injections and using drugs with mild antiviral activity. After much deliberation and praying, it worked! Kris became virus free. This by itself was a miracle; however, her brain had already experienced serious injury from the virus. Her fine and gross motor skills, balance, and speech were still impaired, and she was unable to walk. The virus was gone, but her conditioned remained.

Undaunted, Kris was determined to recover and one day, walk again. She underwent extensive physical, occupational, and speech therapy and was proactive in exploring innovative alternative therapies to help heal her injury, like electromagnetic therapy and hyperbaric oxygen chamber therapy to help stimulate and re-energize the neurons in her brain. She showed incredible resolve, resiliency, and courage during her illness, fighting her battle every day and never giving up. After a brief period of improvement in her physical strength and mental spirit, the virus returned and Kris unfortunately was not able to overcome it a second time. She passed away on November 6, 2011 at age 47.

Kris had the highest of standards. She was a wife, sister, daughter, friend, and nurse. But most of all, she was a mother. She is an inspiration to everyone who knew her, and her story is one we can all learn from and apply to our own lives. Not only did Kris work toward excellence in her life, she helped countless others do the same, even as she worked toward something many of us take for granted—our health.

LESSONS ON EXCELLENCE — *PERSEVERANCE*

Rocky Balboa, played by Sylvester Stallone, is one of our culture's most respected movie heroes. He epitomized perseverance to its core in the way he fought and the way he trained. His most famous speech from the original *Rocky* motion picture is what perseverance is all about. Here is the essence:

> You, me, or nobody is going to hit as hard as life. But it ain't about how hard you're hit. It's about

how hard you can get hit and keep moving forward. How much you can take and keep moving forward. That's how winning is done...You've gotta be willing to take the hits. And not pointing fingers saying you ain't where you want to be because of him, or her, or anybody. Cowards do that and that ain't you. You're better than that!

Cue soundtrack now.

THE NEXT STEP —

1. Do you give up easily, or do you have the inner strength to keep going when things get tough?

2. Compare how you respond to success with how you respond to failure.

3. Name one lesson from Jimmy V's speech that can help you practice perseverance.

4. Who in your life are pillars of courage, determination, and perseverance? What can you learn from their stories?

AFTERWORD

Look for people who will aim for the remarkable, who will not settle for the routine.

David Ogilvy, advertising executive

My goal in writing this book is to add value to your life. By adding value to your life, value is added to my life, and that is why I continue to write. That is the value of adding value. I don't know about you, but when I am not reading a book that gets my juices going, I feel lost. For me, a good book is like a compass, and without one, my thoughts and motivation wander.

One of the reasons I decided to write a book about excellence is because there are not many books written about it. While there are hundreds of books on leadership, management, and success, the topic of excellence remains somewhat elusive. I hope that by breaking down the eight values in *Working Toward Excellence,* you now have a better understanding and appreciation for what it takes to get there. I am also hopeful that the stories, quotes, and wisdom of so many successful people have provided you with the inspiration and motivation to reach your full potential.

One of my biggest role models in this book is Michael Jordan. Growing up in the Chicago area, I watched him lead the Chicago Bulls to six NBA championships. It was an incredible time to be a Chicago sports fan, a stretch I hoped would never end. To me, MJ personified excellence and exemplified the hunger, effort, process, quality, consistency, leadership, time, and perseverance that molded him into becoming the best basketball player in the world and one of the most famous and accomplished athletes in history. So what does this mean for mere mortals like you and I? The good news is that you do not have to be the Michael Jordan of your profession to be successful.

Excellence is a quest all of us can and should undertake. It is a never-ending journey that provides meaning in our lives. It is a noble pursuit that just happens to be valued and rewarded. But more than anything, excellence is a mindset that applies to any and every endeavor, regardless of who you are or what you do. Martin Luther King Jr. said, "If a man is called to be a street sweeper, he should sweep streets even as Michelangelo painted, or Beethoven composed music, or Shakespeare wrote poetry. He should sweep streets so well that all the hosts of heaven and earth will pause to say, here lived a great street sweeper who did his job well."

Sweep your street to the best of your ability, and don't settle for less. Adding value to those driving through is what life is all about.

WORKING TOWARD EXCELLENCE
EVALUATION

This evaluation is designed to help you measure the eight values for achieving excellence and uncommon success in work and life. It requires you to be honest with yourself and become aware of your strengths and weaknesses. As we read from Plato in the Introduction, "Excellent things are rare," so don't be discouraged. Excellence is hard—and is supposed to be! That is why it is so compelling and worthy of pursuit. This evaluation is based on ideas and philosophies found in *Working Toward Excellence* and is a tool for personal growth and improvement, helping you and your organization reach your full potential.

1 = Strongly Disagree
2 = Disagree
3 = Agree
4 = Strongly Agree

Value 1: HUNGER

1. I have a relentless desire and passion
   to achieve excellence. _____

2. I am proactive and take responsibility
   for my life, making no excuses. _____

3. I believe that the secret to my success
   is determined by my daily agenda. _____

4. I am self-motivated and set my own
   bar and standards of success. _____

Value 2: EFFORT

5. I work at my highest capacity, fully
   engaged, totally focused, and completely
   absorbed. _____

6. I believe hard work, not talent, is the
   key to attaining excellence. _____

7. I work to develop mental skills such as
   visualization, along with physical skills. _____

8. I excel at achievement, execution,
   and producing results. _____

Value 3: PROCESS

9. I believe our society tends to overvalue
   results and undervalue process. _____

10. I work to improve my starting point
    by making some progress every day. _____

11. I take time to crockpot the process,
    not microwave it. _____

12. I am devoted to deliberate, purposeful
    practice to achieve excellence.   _____

Value 4: QUALITY

13. I am committed to stamping a superior
    quality upon everything that goes out
    of my hands.   _____
14. I strive to achieve a high performance
    level in everything I do.   _____
15. I have earned the right to be confident
    through detailed preparation.   _____
16. I consider myself a professional and
    come prepared to play every day.   _____

Value 5: CONSISTENCY

17. I do my job extremely well, every
    single time.   _____
18. I have the self-discipline to value
    and embrace repetition.   _____
19. I do not rely on a Hail Mary or
    last-second field goal as a game
    plan for success.   _____
20. I make small, smart choices and
    decisions that add up over time.   _____

Value 6: LEADERSHIP

21. I believe leadership isn't how far we
    advance ourselves, but how far we
    advance others.   _____

22. I believe the performance of an
    organization is the ultimate measure
    of its leader.   _____
23. I build relationships by putting others
    first, listening to them, and treating
    them with respect.   _____
24. I am a person of character, competence,
    commitment, caring, confidence,
    communication and consistency.   _____

Value 7: TIME

25. I tend to pay now and play later, rather
    than play now and pay later.   _____
26. I am not afraid to say no in order to
    value and protect my time.   _____
27. I believe biting off more than I can
    chew will lead to mediocrity.   _____
28. I am punctual, have a planner, value
    every minute, start and end on time,
    and mind the clock.   _____

Value 8: PERSEVERANCE

29. I believe each and every one of us must
    develop perseverance to be successful.   _____
30. I don't give up and have the inner
    strength to keep going when things
    get tough.   _____

31. I have learned to expect adversity and
    will not let it deter me from my goals.   _____

32. I am able to respond to both success
    and failure and continue working
    toward excellence.   _____

RATING SCALE

When you are finished, add up the score for each individual value in the margin. Then add the totals for the eight values together to get your Total Score on the Evaluation.

Total Score_____Rating_____

SCORE	RATING	COMMENTS
110–128	Excellent	Congratulations! You are achieving excellence and uncommon success.
84–109	Good	You are producing good work. To achieve excellence, keep working to improve the items receiving a score of 3 or lower.
58–83	Mediocre	You are producing mediocre work. To improve, practice and develop each of the eight values and raise your scores.
32–57	Poor	Your work is unacceptable. If you want to succeed, reevaluate your goals and make a commitment to working toward excellence, one value at a time.

Individual Value Scores

Break down the eight values in terms of strengths and weaknesses. For example, a 15 on effort and a 10 on time means you have a strong work ethic but tend to procrastinate. A 12 on quality and a 9 on leadership means you should take more pride in your performance level and do a better job building relationships.

14–16	Excellent
11–13	Good
8–10	Mediocre
4–7	Poor

Adapted from *Championship Team Building*,
by Jeff Janssen

BIBLIOGRAPHY

"Augusta National, Billy Payne, Bobby Jones, and Expectations." Hole in the Hull. April 2010. www.holein-thehull.com.

Buyer, Paul. *Marching Bands and Drumlines*. Meredith Music Publications, 2009.

Buyer, Paul. "Mental Training in Percussion." *Percussive Notes* 46, no. 5 (October 2008): 60–61.

Buyer, Paul. "Reading Is Not Optional." *Percussive Notes* 45, no. 3 (June 2007): 34–36.

Buyer, Paul. "Teaching the Values of Competition." *Teaching Music* 13, no. 1 (August 2005): 28–31.

Calloway, Joe. *Becoming a Category of One, 2nd Edition*. John Wiley and Sons, 2009.

Coates, Dennis and Meredith Bell. *Strong for Leadership*. Performance Support Systems, 2010.

Collins English Dictionary. HarperCollins, 2003.

Collins, Jim. *Good to Great and the Social Sectors*. HarperCollins, 2005.

Colvin, Geoffrey. "What It Takes to Be Great," *Fortune* 154, no. 9 (October 2006): 88–96.

Covey, Stephen. *The Leader in Me*. Free Press, 2008.

Covey, Stephen. *The Seven Habits of Highly Effective People*. Free Press, 2004.

Covey, Stephen. *The Seven Habits of Highly Effective People Personal Workbook*. Fireside, 2003.

Gorrie, Jon. *Performing in the Zone*. CreateSpace, 2009.

Hamm, John. *Unusually Excellent*. Jossey-Bass, 2011.

Hansson, David Heinemeier. "Saying No." *SUCCESS Magazine* (July 2011). CD-ROM.

Hardy, Darren. *The Compound Effect*. Success Books, 2010.

Hendricks, Gay. *The Centered Athlete*. Prentice-Hall, 1982.

Hirschhorn, Doug. *8 Ways to Great*. Penguin Group, 2009.

Janssen, Jeff. *Championship Team Building*. Janssen Peak Performance, Inc., 1999.

Janssen, Jeff and Greg Dale. *The Seven Secrets of Successful Coaches*. Janssen Peak Performance, Inc., 2002.

Johnson, Ted. "The Masters: 10 Things They Don't Tell You about Augusta National on TV." April 4, 2011. www.bleacherreport.com.

"Kobe Bryant...God-Given Gift or Work Ethic?" Pakistan Basketball. March 15, 2010. www.pakistanbasketball.com.

Kruger, Lon. *The Xs & Os of Success*. Stephens Press, 2009.

Krzyzewski, Mike. *Beyond Basketball*. Warner Books, 2006.

Latta, Jonathan. "I've Been Hired as a College Percussion Instructor: What Now?" *Percussive Notes* 47, no. 3 (2009): 20–23.

Lombardi Jr., Vince. *What It Takes to Be #1*. McGraw-Hill, 2001.

Mack, Gary. *Mind Gym*. Contemporary Books/McGraw-Hill, 2001.

Maxwell, John C. "Leadership Landmines." *SUCCESS Magazine* (July 2011): 18–19.

Maxwell, John C. *The 21 Irrefutable Laws of Leadership, 10th Anniversary Edition*. Thomas Nelson, 2007.

Maxwell, John C. *Today Matters*. Warner Books, 2004.

Nater, Swen. *You Haven't Taught Until They Have Learned*. Fitness Information Technology, 2010.

Phillips, Donald T. *Run to Win*. St. Martin's Griffin, 2001.

Pink, Daniel. *Drive: The Surprising Truth About What Motivates Us*. Riverhead Trade, 2011.

Pirsig, Robert. *Zen and the Art of Motorcycle Maintenance*. HarperCollins. 1974.

Reinhard, Keith. Quoted in Ted Kurland Associates' "Innovation and Jazz: A Talk with Wynton Marsalis." www.tedkurland.com/materials/onesheets/ MarsalisWyntonInnovations.pdf.

Robbins. Mel. "The Time Is Now." *SUCCESS Magazine* (December 2010): 18.

Safer, Morley. "Wynton Marsalis." CBS' *60 Minutes*. June 26, 2011.

Schwartz, Larry. "Michael Jordan Transcends Hoops." 2007. http://ESPN.com.

Sharma, Robin. "The Picasso Story." *SUCCESS Magazine* (April 2010). CD-ROM.

Spizman, Justin and Robyn Spizman. *Don't Give Up... Don't Ever Give Up*. Sourcebooks, 2010.

Sterner, Thomas M. *The Practicing Mind*. Mountain Sage Publishing, 2005.

Syed, Matthew. *Bounce*. HarperCollins Publishers, 2010.

Weckl, Dave. *Synergy*. Audio CD. Stretch Records, 1999.

Wikipedia. www.wikipedia.org.

Williams, Pat. *Daly Wisdom*. Advantage Media Group, Inc., 2010.

Williams, Pat. *How to Be Like Mike.* Health Communications, Inc., 2001.

Williams, Pat and Jim Denney. *Extreme Focus.* Health Communications, Inc., 2011.

Winder, Richard and Daniel Judd. "Quality: How Do You Define It?" *Quality Digest.* 2001. www.qualitydigest.com.

Wooden, John and Steve Jamison. *Coach Wooden's Leadership Game Plan for Success.* McGraw-Hill, 2009.

Wooden, John and Steve Jamison. *The Essential Wooden.* McGraw-Hill, 2007.

Yamada, Kobi. *Commitment to Excellence.* Compendium Publishing, 2003.

ABOUT THE AUTHOR

Paul Buyer is Director of Percussion, Director of Music, and Professor of Music at Clemson University. He received his Doctor of Musical Arts and Master of Music degrees from the University of Arizona and his Bachelor of Science degree from Ball State University. Dr. Buyer's first book, *Marching Bands and Drumlines: Secrets of Success from the Best of the Best,* is published by Meredith Music Publications and exclusively distributed by the Hal Leonard Corporation. He is a contributing author to the second edition of *Teaching Percussion* by Gary Cook, and his articles have appeared in *American Music Teacher, Teaching Music*, and *Percussive Notes*. Dr. Buyer's writing and teaching focus on what it takes to achieve excellence. He lives with his wife April in Central, South Carolina. His website is www.paulbuyer.com.

BUY A SHARE OF THE FUTURE IN YOUR COMMUNITY

These certificates make great holiday, graduation and birthday gifts that can be personalized with the recipient's name. The cost of one S.H.A.R.E. or one square foot is $54.17. The personalized certificate is suitable for framing and will state the number of shares purchased and the amount of each share, as well as the recipient's name. The home that you participate in "building" will last for many years and will continue to grow in value.

Here is a sample SHARE certificate:

HABITAT FOR HUMANITY

THIS CERTIFIES THAT

YOUR NAME HERE

HAS INVESTED IN A HOME FOR A DESERVING FAMILY

1985-2010

TWENTY-FIVE YEARS OF BUILDING FUTURES
IN OUR COMMUNITY ONE HOME AT A TIME

1200 SQUARE FOOT HOUSE @ $65,000 = $54.17 PER SQUARE FOOT
This certificate represents a tax-deductible donation. It has no cash value

YES, I WOULD LIKE TO HELP!

I support the work that Habitat for Humanity does and I want to be part of the excitement! As a donor, I will receive periodic updates on your construction activities but, more importantly, I know my gift will help a family in our community realize the dream of homeownership. **I would like to SHARE in your efforts against substandard housing in my community!** *(Please print below)*

PLEASE SEND ME _____ SHARES at $54.17 EACH = $ $_____

In Honor Of: _____

Occasion: (Circle One)   HOLIDAY   BIRTHDAY   ANNIVERSARY

     OTHER: _____

Address of Recipient: _____

Gift From: _____ *Donor Address:* _____

Donor Email: _____

I AM ENCLOSING A CHECK FOR $ $_____ **PAYABLE TO HABITAT FOR HUMANITY OR PLEASE CHARGE MY VISA OR MASTERCARD** *(CIRCLE ONE)*

Card Number _____ Expiration Date: _____

Name as it appears on Credit Card _____ Charge Amount S _____

Signature _____

Billing Address _____

Telephone # Day _____ Eve _____

PLEASE NOTE: Your contribution is tax-deductible to the fullest extent allowed by law.
Habitat for Humanity • P.O. Box 1443 • Newport News, VA 23601 • 757-596-5553
www.HelpHabitatforHumanity.org

CPSIA information can be obtained
at www.ICGtesting.com
Printed in the USA
FFOW02n0509160814
6916FF